BERRIES

Reaktion's Botanical series is the first of its kind, integrating horticultural and botanical writing with a broader account of the cultural and social impact of trees, plants and flowers.

Published
Apple Marcia Reiss
Bamboo Susanne Lucas
Berries Victoria Dickenson
Birch Anna Lewington
Cactus Dan Torre
Cannabis Chris Duvall
Carnation Twigs Way
Carnivorous Plants Dan Torre
Chrysanthemum Twigs Way
Geranium Kasia Boddy
Grasses Stephen A. Harris
Lily Marcia Reiss
Mulberry Peter Coles
Oak Peter Young
Palm Fred Gray
Pine Laura Mason
Poppy Andrew Lack
Primrose Elizabeth Lawson
Rhododendron Richard Milne
Rose Catherine Horwood
Snowdrop Gail Harland
Sunflowers Stephen A. Harris
Tulip Celia Fisher
Weeds Nina Edwards
Willow Alison Syme
Yew Fred Hageneder

BERRIES

Victoria Dickenson

REAKTION BOOKS

*To my husband Jeff Harrison, who has spent many afternoons in
companionable gathering of the sweet fruits of field and garden*

Published by
REAKTION BOOKS LTD
Unit 32, Waterside
44–48 Wharf Road
London N1 7UX, UK

www.reaktionbooks.co.uk

First published 2020
Copyright © Victoria Dickenson 2020

Printed and bound in India by Replika Press Pvt. Ltd

A catalogue record for this book is available from the British Library

ISBN 978 1 78914 193 1

Contents

꧁

Preface *7*

one Berries True and False *11*

two Berries in Mind *43*

three Berries in the Hand *71*

four Garden Varieties *97*

five Preserving the Harvest *127*

six The Global Berry *156*

Timeline *177*
References *181*
Select Bibliography *197*
Associations and Websites *199*
Acknowledgements *201*
Photo Acknowledgements *202*
Index *204*

Wild arctic berries, Alaska.

Preface

𓎛

I can think of no finer way to spend a late summer's day than on the high coastal barrens of Newfoundland, that rocky outlier of the North Atlantic, picking blueberries. Amid the spice-box smells of juniper and balsam, I crouch to find clusters of small, deeply blue berries among shiny green leaves. A constant wind thrums through the trees, gulls shriek, and the fruit plops roundly into the bucket. These are not the large watery berries of commercial blueberry farms – highbush plants, shaken, raked and mechanically sorted. These are dark flavoured and hard won, each firm berry rolled from its stem by hand. They make delicious pies and royal purple jam, fragrant with the savage scent of wild lands.

I am not alone in my admiration of blueberries and the intense experience of picking in the wild. Writing towards the end of his life, Henry David Thoreau, the celebrated American naturalist and author, could remember the marvel of a day when, decades earlier, he stumbled onto a rich patch:

> I can still see in my mind the beautiful clusters of these berries as they appeared to me twenty or thirty years ago, when I came upon an undiscovered bed of them behind some higher bushes in a sproutland – the rich clusters drooping in the shade there and bluing all the ground, without a grain of their blue disturbed. It was a thrilling discovery to find such ethereal fruits under the still, fresh green of oaks and hickory sprouts.[1]

In his fictionalized memoir, Ray Bradbury, the author of *The Martian Chronicles* (1950), wrote about a strange and unnervingly visceral childhood experience much closer to home. Picking not blueberries but purple fox grapes, 'his fingers sink through green shadow and come forth stained with such colour that it seemed he had somehow cut the forest and delved his hand in the open wound.'[2]

What is it about the small fruits of field and wood that encourage rapture? These gifts of the earth – flagrant in hedgerows, trailing along footpaths, carpeting the forest floor or colouring the uplands – are so ubiquitous as to be commonplace and so extraordinary that they permeate myths, legends, folktales and poetry. These are the soft fruits of an English summer, *les petits fruits des champs* of the French countryside, the hidden delights that Thoreau extolled. We are blessed with an extravagant global cornucopia of these sweet, fragile productions. Strawberries, blueberries, bilberries, huckleberries, raspberries and blackberries (and their lesser-known cousins the

Elizabeth Adela Forbes, *Blackberry Gathering*, c. 1912, oil on canvas.

Raspberries, c. 1874, chromolithograph.

Raspberries.

dewberries, thimbleberries and salmonberries), frost-ripened cranberries, red and black currants and, of course, green gooseberries, but
also partridge berries and crowberries (as if only birds fancied
them), scarlet cracker berries, pure-white snowberries, the strange
blue haskap of the honeysuckle and golden-orange cloudberries –
they stain our fingers and strain our backs in the gathering. There
are the berries we pluck from trees and shrubs – purple mulberries,
elderberries, dogberries, saskatoons, and chokeberries, the *madroño*
that apes the strawberry. And then there are what Thoreau called
the 'far-fetched fruits' of tropical climes, more recently arrived in

the international berry market – açai and goji berries and Chinese gooseberries, the kiwifruits of New Zealand. Berries are botanically confusing, horticulturally complex and almost uniformly delicious – truly the first fruits of the earth.

one

Berries True and False

𝔁

To the botanist, a berry is any multi-seeded fruit without a stone that grows from a single flower. For most of us, enamoured of these vegetable gifts, any round, sweet fruit is termed a berry. Grapes are archetypal berries, delicious glistening globes with tiny seeds; indeed, in Old English they were called 'wine berries' (*win-berige*). Carolus Linnaeus, the eighteenth-century naturalist who founded modern taxonomy and systems of classification, recognized eight different kinds of fruits, 'bacca' or berries among them.[1] 'Baccae', from the Latin word for berries, is still used by botanists to describe the 'true berries' group, some of whose members bear no resemblance to the popular image of a berry. While it is possible for most of us to see the red fruits of the coffee plant and the tomato as berries, it is much harder to think of bananas in the same class as blueberries. The long, thick-skinned fruits clustered in great green bunches are, however, true berries. Cucumbers, pumpkins and watermelons also seem very far from the fragile, finger-staining fruits of the fields, but they too are botanical berries, their fruit termed a 'pepo'. Like all berries, they are indehiscent, in that they lack a defined seam or 'line of weakness' along which the fruit splits, unlike, say, a pea pod. True berries have small seeds encased in juicy flesh; some we happily swallow, while others are large enough to stick in our teeth or our throats. We ignore the tiny seeds in bananas or blueberries but spit out the pips of oranges – yet another member of the berry clan. Citrus fruits have noticeably thickened rinds, but berries they are, and their group was given the name 'hesperidium' by a nineteenth-century French botanist, an allusion to the golden apples of the Hesperides, the wondrous fruit that glowed on the tree guarded by the Nymphs of Evening.[2]

Whether called baccae, pepo or hesperidium, true berries develop from the ovary of a single flower, but even here the botanical

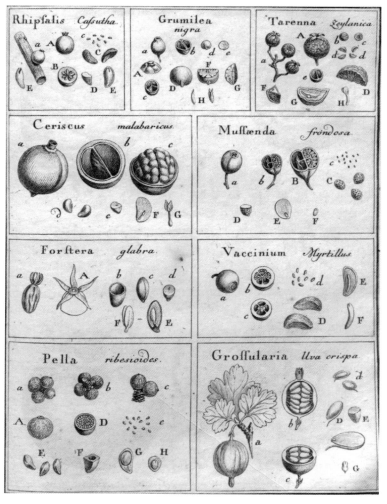

Variety of fruits classified as 'bacca' in Joseph Gaertner's *De fructibus et seminibus plantarum* (1788).

Musk strawberry (*Fragaria moschata*), showing achenes.

classification is murky. Ovaries can be superior or inferior. In berries that develop from an inferior ovary, such as the blueberry, the floral tube (the elongated cup of the flower that contains the ovary and sports sepals and petals) can become fleshy. And while the blueberry would seem to be the very definition of a berry, due to this miscegenation botanists persist in calling it a 'false berry'. What is even more surprising is that many of what we think of as everyday berries are not really berries at all. The strawberry, arguably the most storied of berries, is an 'accessory' fruit, its tiny seeds, or achenes, embedded on the surface of the sweet red flesh that develops not from the ovary of the female flower, but from surrounding tissue. Some of what we commonly call berries are actually drupes. Drupes are the classic stone fruits, such as peaches and plums; bayberries, the waxy fruits of aromatic myrtles found along the shores of eastern North America, are classic drupes – thin skin, fleshy interior and hard shell (endocarp) protecting the seed. Avocados are either true berries or true drupes, depending on which authority you consult, and to add to the confusion, the blackberry, beloved of children, is an aggregation of drupelets. Each juicy cell of the blackberry has developed from a separate ovary of the same flower, clustered together into what scientists call an etaerio of drupelets, a dark and delicious association. Mulberries, which might be supposed at first glance kin to blackberries, are no such thing. They are multiple fruits and each tiny globular section is the child of a different flower, fused into a single entity.

The problem of discerning by eye alone what is a 'berry' is not a problem for foragers and gardeners, who classify berries almost solely by their appearance and gustatory qualities. It is a problem for botanists, who have difficulty not only in agreeing on fruit types, and which fruits belong in which category, but in using the offspring of the flower to establish natural relationships between species. Linnaeus wisely based his botanical taxonomies on flowers, which though ephemeral, seem a more trustworthy guide to discerning natural relationships among plants. Fruits, on the other hand, which may look remarkably similar in outward appearance, occur across a broad spectrum of plants from widely differing families, and even from different taxa. The fruits of mulberries (Moraceae) and blackberries (Rosaceae), both members of the great Rosales order (whose type family is, not surprisingly, the roses), are superficially very similar. In Spanish, *la mora* is used for both, though they come from taxonomically distinct families.[3] This confusion of scientific and popular names highlights the long history we as a species have had with berries, true or false. Plants, our cohabitants of the biosphere, have cunningly developed juicy, edible berries to enlist hungry birds and sweet-toothed mammals in seed dispersal, and by this stratagem, our vegetable universe is immeasurably richer.

The Evolution of Berries

In 1877 Alfred Russel Wallace, the British naturalist who, with Charles Darwin, defined the principles of natural selection, mused on the significance of colour in fruits:

But flowers and fruits exhibit definite and well-pronounced tints, often varying from species to species, and more or less clearly related to the habits and functions of the plant. With the few exceptions already pointed out, these may be generally classed as *attractive* colours. The seeds of plants require to be dispersed so as to reach places favourable for germination and growth . . . But there is a large class of seeds which . . . are mostly contained in eatable fruits. These fruits are devoured by birds or beasts, and the hard seeds pass through their stomachs undigested, and, owing probably to the gentle heat and moisture to which they have been subjected, in a condition highly favourable for germination.

As Wallace noted, though the apple falls not far from the tree, this may not be the best reproductive strategy for a plant. Better that the seed be dispersed at some distance from the parent, to permit optimal growth. Some seeds are blown by the wind but others must rely on their more mobile coevolutionists. Based on his observations in South America, Malaysia and Britain, Wallace theorized that fruits were brightly coloured so they might attract animals to aid in distributing fruits and their seeds far and wide:

> the eatable fruits almost invariably acquire a bright colour as they ripen, while at the same time they become soft and often full of agreeable juices. Our red haws and hips, our black elderberries, our blue sloes and whortleberries, our white mistletoe and snowberry, and our orange sea-buckthorn, are examples of the colour-sign of edibility; and in every part of the world the same phenomenon is found . . . there is probably nowhere a brightly-coloured pulpy fruit which does not serve as food for some species of bird or mammal.[4]

When Wallace wrote about the attractive colouration of fruit, he was affirming the significance of colour as an important evolutionary

Katsushika Hokusai, *Mozu ruri yuki-no-shita hebi-ichigo* (Shrike, Red-flanked Bluetail, Saxifrage and Wild Strawberry), *c.* 1834, woodblock print.

trait, something that many prior observers had dismissed. A century later, scientists started to study in more detail how the behaviour of frugivores – birds, bats and primates – could select for certain characteristics in fruits, and how fruits adapted to ensure their delectability to a broad spectrum of animal 'helpers'. The mutualism of fruits and frugivores is the product of diffuse coevolution over time;

it is also an example of communication between two kingdoms so widely separated that we might think such an exchange impossible.

How we and other animals perceive colour in berries and other fruits is the result of three factors: the reflectance of the surface of the fruit, the ambient light and the sensory physiology of the viewer. Berries are coloured by three different pigments, and the colours they produce are also affected by the properties of the skin and, in certain fruits, by its waxiness. Some blueberries and grapes have a frosty blush, while others are deepest blue-black. Deep reds, blues, black and purple are the colours created by anthocyanin; yellow, orange and red are the products of carotenoids, and green derives from chlorophyll. Some red fruits are also coloured by anthocyanin (strawberries, for example), while others are tinted the more orangey red of carotenoids (like tomatoes). As many fruits ripen, the levels of chlorophyll decrease, and fruits go from yellow to orange to red, and in many cases to black. The deeper the colour, the riper the fruit; blackberries are 'green' when 'red' and sea buckthorn is hard when yellow, soft when orange. Colour is the cue that signals to an animal, 'I am good to eat.' Birds and beasts learn that in most cases dark colours mean ripe, juicy berries, and they select those that promise the sweetest treats, helpfully spreading the seeds throughout their territories. Colour can also ensure that a berry is conspicuous against green leaves, though this may be more important for birds than for bats and primates, the chief frugivores among mammals. Birds, in fact, prefer blue, black or deep red fruits, easy to see against background foliage. Foraging primates are partial to green fruits, like gooseberries and avocados or other tropical fruits that ripen in the understorey of thick forests. Nocturnal fruit-eating bats are more attracted by scent than colour. Recent studies of the local plant community and certain small birds in Spain have revealed the success of this colour-coded communication strategy. Blackcaps (*Sylvia atricapilla*) and garden warblers (*Sylvia borin*) consistently choose the deepest-hued berries, which happen to be those with the most lipid content. Lipids are fats, and birds need them to survive winter conditions or long-distance

Ellen Thayer Fisher, *Blackberries*, 1887, chromolithograph.

migrations. The anthocyanin pigment signals the presence of lipids, and these birds have learned to read the signals.[5]

Colour is not the only characteristic of fruit affected by the conversation between immobile plants and their animal helpers. Size, shape and the proportion of delicious flesh to seed have been matters of negotiation. Bats, birds and primates (including the human species) are nibblers, mashers or gulpers. Bats tend to nibble

Kathryn Ball, *Viscum album* (Mistletoe), 2000, watercolour.

or mash. Depending on the size of the fruit, and the size of the animal, birds or primates will take little bites, grind and mash, or eat the fruit whole. It is not advantageous for a plant if too many of its dispersal agents sit on its branches or under its shade, spitting out the seeds in situ. It is preferable that the seeds be tiny and be consumed with the flesh, that they be gluey and stick to the beak, or that they be large and surrounded by nutritious flesh that is very attractive to gulpers. Very few of us attempt to strain the seeds of raspberries, blueberries or strawberries through our teeth. It is far easier to enjoy the succulent berry whole and excrete the seeds later in a different location, fulfilling the objective of the plants. The humble crowberry of the northern tundra is an obvious success at this interchange of services. Two closely related species of crowberries (*Empetrum* sp.) grow at opposite ends of the globe – *E. nigrum* in Canada, Alaska, Iceland and Greenland, and *E. rubrum* in Patagonia and the Falkland Islands – and almost nowhere in between. The most parsimonious explanation found by biologists for this extreme distribution is the migration of berry-loving mid-Pleistocene birds. Like today's whimbrels and golden plovers, they flew each year between the ends of the earth, crops full of crowberries.[6] The mistletoe (*Viscum* sp.) adopts another strategy: its seed is encased in a fleshy berry (botanically a drupe) and coated with a sticky layer of viscin. Birds such as European mistle thrushes (*Turdus viscivorus*), who specialize in eating mistletoe berries, squeeze the seed out of the flesh as they eat. The viscous seed adheres to the beak, and when a fastidious thrush wipes her beak on a branch the seed sticks to the bark and a new mistletoe plant has found a home. (Human foragers also used mistletoe berries to make gluey birdlime, which, when spread along a branch, may have caught mistle thrushes.) Gulpers, such as giant cassowaries, who have been observed eating seven papayas at one sitting, swallow their fruit whole, seeds and all.[7] Other gulpers such as hornbills can carry a number of fruits in their throat pouches, to be enjoyed later at some distance from the fruiting tree. In a similar way, fruit pigeons retain the seeds in their guts for a number of hours while they fly to distant perches, where they release their burden in new terrain.

Bats are not the only creatures attracted to the scent of ripe fruits. Human nostrils can also evaluate ripeness in the wafting perfume of berries. We are instructed to sniff at melons to determine ripeness, and a patch of glowing red strawberries can be particularly fragrant.[8] Recent studies suggest that this olfactory conspicuousness – the substantial shift in odour profile signalling ripeness – may have evolved specifically to convey information ('Eat me!') to mammals.[9] There are also subtler scents to which mammals are attuned. An ethanol 'plume' develops above a mass of ripening fruit, and even at low levels can be sensed by nearby primates (and by insects, as anyone who has brought home a vigorous crowd of fruit flies with ripe bananas knows). Ethanol correlates with the sugar content of fruit, and we and our primate relatives have a sweet tooth. So it seems does the agouti, a Central and South American rodent, which gulps its fruit and is responsible for the reproductive success of a particular species of palm. When the sweet, ethanol-fragrant berries of the black palm (*Astrocaryum standleyanum*) fall to the ground, the agouti sniffs them out and, undeterred by the large seed, thriftily carries the berries away to cache for a later meal. Buried in the earth, and often forgotten by the agouti, the palm seeds are in an optimal environment to produce new seedlings, at some distance from the parent tree.[10] While there are reports of drunken birds crashing into windows and wobbling on branches, avian ethanol consumption may be accidental. In late winter and early spring in North America, the native cedar waxwings and robins are attracted to the bright clusters of blackberries, rowan and juniper berries that remain on bushes and trees from autumn. Fermentation in the thawing berries turns their sugar into alcohol, and over-consumption can lead to unfortunate results for the birds. Cedar waxwings are almost exclusively fruit eaters, and their livers are consequently large, to deal with their sometimes alcoholic repasts. There are, however, cases in which too many berries, stored in their extendible throats, continue to ferment and tax even their ability to remain sober, leading to drunkenness and death – not the desired result of mutualism between fruit and frugivore.[11]

The Great Berry Families

While our primate ancestors played a role in selecting for delectability in berries, we continue to make very deliberate choices about the berries we prefer and those we do not. The 'small fruits' that we gather, tend, pick and increasingly ship from one side of the globe to the other are categorized as the horticultural berries. Strictly speaking, horticulture refers to the cultivation of the garden, but with berries, the garden extends into the open heath, a hedgerow or a mossy wood, as the berry-loving Henry David Thoreau clearly pointed out:

> Thus, any summer, after spending the forenoon in your chamber reading or writing, in the afternoon you walk forth into the fields and woods, and turn aside, if you please, into some rich, withdrawn, and untrodden swamp, and find there bilberries large and fair awaiting you in inexhaustible abundance. This is your real garden.[12]

Some wild berries have been brought within the garden proper, and improved through cultivation and breeding over time, while others have resisted domestication, or are so freely available as to make gathering the preferred method of harvest. The berries that we human frugivores have selected and now sell in the stalls and supermarkets of the global berry market from Beijing to Bristol, are the wildly diverse productions of the great green world of the angiosperms, or flowering plants. Berries are not the unique discovery of a single branch of flowering plants. Along their long evolutionary ways, many different plants from widely varying ancestors have found the berry a useful device in which to pack seeds to ensure wide distribution and successful germination. The majority, however, belong to two large groupings of flowering plants, the rosids and the asterids. It is as if the edible berry world can be divided between the fruits of the roses and daisies (though berberries or barberries derive from the distinct order of the buttercups, the Ranunculales). Fruits that we call berries are also produced by plants that are members of a completely different clade. A clade is a group of organisms with a common ancestor, and the roses, asters and buttercups all derive from ancestral flowering plants of the eudicotyledon clade. Bananas (true berries in the botanical sense and linked to gingers in a grand Zingiberales order) and the newly fashionable açai berry (the fruit of a palm in the order Arecales) are both monocotyledons, within the same clade as the orchids, the lilies and the arums.[13]

A Rose by Any Other Name

Within the rosids are different orders of berry-bearing plants, including those of the two groupings pepo and hesperidium, whose modified berries we know better as melons and citrus. The pepos include not only melons but cucumbers, gourds, watermelons and the world's largest berry – the pumpkin.[14] The hesperidiums are the traditional citrus fruits – oranges, lemons and limes – as well as tangerines, pomelos, grapefruits, kumquats, kuzu and mandarins.[15] Among the rosids are also numbered the fruits of the vine. Ivies, lianas, creepers and all sorts of trailing, rampant vines with curling tendrils and bunches of berries belong to the order Vitales, but the one that we as a species have cultivated most assiduously is the grape, *Vitis vinifera*, native to Europe and southwestern Asia. There are also endemic *Vitis* species in North America, with lovely descriptive names – Frost or Riverbank, Summer, Rock, Muscadine and Fox. The Riverbank grape (*V. riparia*) was likely the vine running riot over the new-found lands across the sea that the Viking explorer Eric the Red named Vinland. The Fox grape (*V. labrusca*), also familiar to North Americans as the Concord grape, was equally a promise of abundance to the early European settlers of the eastern seaboard. Unfortunately, with its 'foxy' earthy taste, it proved a disappointment to those who craved the familiar vintages of their home terroirs. These three berry families are the legendary fruits of fertility in the European imagination. Overflowing cornucopias of lustrous grapes, juicy oranges with peel curling away from glistening flesh and melons split to reveal their luminous erotic interiors, bestrew the canvases of countless still-life and allegorical paintings. These berries have been the subject of so many treatises, books and poems that this book is dedicated to the humbler fruits of field and forest, the small sweet juicy offspring of bush, branch and earth.

The members of the Rose family itself (Rosaceae in the order Rosales) have evidently evolved in close relation to the human species, given our delight in the perfume and taste of their fruits. Apples, peaches, pears and plums – all are roses at heart. The family also embraces some of our best-known and most widely grown berries, even if, in fact, they are not botanically 'true berries'. Strawberries (*Fragaria* sp.), which are accessory fruits or etaeria of achenes, and blackberries and raspberries (both *Rubus* sp.), which are associations of drupelets, are the gastronomic trinity of the family. They have worldwide distribution and grow in all continents, with the exception of Antarctica. They share with the roses the characteristic five-petalled flower, toothed leaves, and in the case of the two closely related *Rubus* cousins, piercing thorns and prickles. Blackberries, in particular, are famously difficult to gather from woods and hedgerows, their bristly canes tearing clothes and scratching bare skin, leaving fingers sticky and stained with dark vegetable blood. The European blackberry or bramble is considered in some areas an invasive species, creating thickets so dense and thorny that it excludes native vegetation and endangers local ecosystems.[16] Strawberries, on the other hand, are a gentler fruit, though they are known to run riot in gardens, throwing out runners with gay abandon to cover the earth with offspring. They were called *streawbergan* in Old English for their habit of growing strewn on the soil or in grassy places, though the etymology of the name is open to some debate. In other European languages, and also in Old Saxon, they are *erthberi*, or earth berry, which seems very appropriate as anyone who, nose close to ground, has picked wild strawberries knows.[17]

Rubus is a complex genus native to the Americas, Europe and Asia, with over a dozen subgenera and hundreds of species, most of which resemble, at least superficially, garden-variety blackberries and raspberries.[18] These two groupings are distinguished one from the other by the simple act of picking. In blackberries, the core remains with the plucked fruit, while in raspberries, it remains on the plant, making the raspberries delicate fruits for shipping and handling. Not all the bramble berries grow on canes, and American dewberries (*R. ursinus*), also known as Pacific blackberry, and several other species grow trailing on the ground, though the European species (*R. caesius*) grows upright. These berries often grow singly (and are hard won in areas with biting flies) rather than in bountiful clusters, which is a happy characteristic of the Japanese wineberry or wine raspberry (*R. phoenicolasius*), also confusingly called dewberry, but distinguished by the sticky hairs that cover the growing berries. Thimbleberries (*R. parviflorus*) are native to North America, and when plucked, the hollow core surrounded by drupelets resembles a thimble. Others that share this characteristic and which we also call thimbleberries are the black raspberry or blackcap (*R. occidentalis*), native to North America, and the roseleaf bramble (*R. rosifolius*), originally native to the Himalayas but now gone wild in Puerto Rico and California. Not all blackberries or raspberries are red or black; salmonberries (*R. spectabilis*), as the name might suggest, vary from gold to orange (they can also be red and black) and were eaten with salmon by Indigenous peoples of the northwest coast of North America. The lovely circumpolar cloudberry (*R. chamaemorus*), much esteemed in Finland and the Scandinavian countries, as well as in Newfoundland and eastern Canada, is an atypical member of the genus.[19] A bright orange-red when green (rather like the blackberry), an orange-gold when ripe and pale gold when soft and overripe, cloudberries huddle close to the ground in wet meadows and boggy peatlands, a single berry to each female plant. Unlike most of their

Henry Fletcher, after Pieter Casteels III, 'June', from *Twelve Months of Fruit* (1732).

congeners, they are dioecious, with both male and female plants required for reproduction. The majority of brambles, however, generally abstain from sex of any kind, the developing egg in the ovary fertilizing itself – a process known as apomixis.[20] Apomixis results in offspring that are genetic clones, which, happily for the gardener, means that all the seeds sown result in plants that preserve the best characteristics of the parent. Gardeners have, however, tinkered with their brambles and created a number of hybrids that are the fruits

After Henry Noel Humphreys, 'Dewberry, Common Bramble or Blackberry, Arctic or Dwarf Crimson Bramble, Cloudberry', coloured lithograph, pl. 32, from Jane Webb Loudon, *British Wild Flowers* (1846).

of crosses between selected *Rubus* species, giving us the unnatural but delectable loganberries, boysenberries, tayberries, marionberries and hildaberries, to name a few. The history of their breeding is recounted in Chapter Four.

Strawberries in nature are somewhat less complicated than their *Rubus* cousins. There are only just over twenty species in the *Fragaria* genus, but they have a much more complex sex life.[21] Wild strawberries are separated into six groups according to the number of chromosomes they possess, varying from fourteen (diploid, or two sets of seven chromosomes) up to seventy (decaploid, or ten sets). *Fragaria vesca*, the European woodland strawberry celebrated in song and poetry since the Middle Ages, and with a worldwide distribution, is diploid, as is the green-fruited strawberry, *F. viridis*. *F. moschata*, the European musk strawberry, known as the 'Hautbois' in England, is the only hexaploid species, with 42 chromosomes. The two western hemisphere natives, *F. chiloensis* from the west coast and *F. virginiana* found on the east coast, are both octoploid (56 chromosomes). Polyploidy (the characteristic of having multiple chromosomes) is generally related to vigour and reproductive success, but in *Fragaria*, the humble diploid *F. vesca* has managed to make its way around the world while some chromosome-heavy species have been confined to more limited areas. *F. iturupensis*, for example, may have up to seventy chromosomes, but it lives only on Iturup in the Kuril Islands between Japan and Russia.

The differing number of chromosomes among strawberries is not simply a botanical curiosity. Polyploidy posed a problem to early plant breeders, who could not understand why crosses between different species would not bear fruit, or if they did produce offspring, why these, in turn, were not fertile. Strawberries are also, and unusually among flowering plants, dioecious, with male and female plants necessary for reproduction (though some species can also bear 'perfect' flowers capable of self-fertilization). Early gardeners often removed the sterile male plants, as they considered them unproductive, with disastrous consequences for their strawberry yield. Breeders have, however, been able to take advantage of the strawberry's sexual dimorphism to cross their best plants, creating a bewildering number of varieties. The most famous cross, however, and one of the earliest, seems to have come about by accident. Two 'New World' strawberries, one from Chile and the other from Virginia, both with eight sets of chromosomes, were brought together by their human keepers in the gardens of France, where they met and mingled their pollen. Philip Miller, the head of the Chelsea Physic Garden, first described their offspring in the 1759 edition of his *Gardener's Dictionary*; by the later eighteenth century, *Fragaria* x *ananassa*, called 'The Pine', was being cultivated in gardens throughout Europe. A large-fruited octoploid like its parents, the berry had the odour and shape of a pineapple, a much-coveted fruit of the period. As a bonus, the hybrid turned out to be a hermaphrodite, breeding true and able to be cultivated from seed. The Pine is the origin of our garden-variety strawberry and another product of the ongoing mutualism between fruits and their human frugivores.

As if blackberries, raspberries and strawberries were not enough, the Rose family also offers us the sweet round 'berries' of trees and shrubs, though like brambles and strawberries, they are not necessarily botanical berries. Rowan or mountain ash; the service- or saskatoon berry; the chokeberry, also known by the much-less-daunting name of aronia; as well as hawberries, hollyberries (an American native after which Hollywood was named), osoberries or Indian plum; and the sloe of sloe gin cling together in a subfamily of roses (Maloideae). Most of these fruits are drupes or pomes (similar to an apple or pear who share this grouping), but their superficial resemblance to the common berries of field or hedgerow encourages us to name them berries. The mulberry is also a rose by another name (or at least a Rosales). The 'berries' of the trees and bushes in the Moraceae family are multiple fruits, white, red or black, depending on their place of origin. The white mulberry (*Morus alba*) is a native of east Asia, the black (*M. nigra*) of southwest Asia and the red (*M. rubra*) of eastern North America, though the gustatory qualities of their fruits and the utility of their leaves (particularly of the white mulberry) as food for silkworms have encouraged their planting worldwide.

Overleaf: Wild strawberry (*Fragaria vesca*). Pakri peninsula, Estonia.

Asters

The familiar asters of garden and field are only the tip of the floral iceberg that is the asterids. Within this great subclass of flowering plants are amaranths, dogweeds, purslanes, pokeweeds, pinks, cacti, buckwheats and, thankfully for berry lovers, the members of the order Ericales, home to the large family of Ericaceae or the heaths, containing at last count 124 genera and over 4,250 species. Like the heathers of the Scottish Highlands, the plants in this family are, for the most part, low-lying plants of heaths and bogs, though some species rear up into small shrubs and trees. All thrive and bring forth their annual bounty on thin acidic soils, thanks to the mutualistic relationship with various mycorrhizal fungi in their root systems that supply the plants with nitrogen in exchange for carbohydrates derived from photosynthesis. This happy symbiosis originated some 140 million years ago, enabling members of the clan to spread their roots on every continent other than Antarctica, and on high, cold ground inhospitable to many other plants. Among the vast array of heathers, heaths, small trees and bushes, there are three groupings whose fruits are sought by human and beast. Blueberries (*Vaccinium* sp.) and their close cousins the huckleberries (*Gaylussacia* sp.) and bilberries (*Vaccinium myrtillus*) are members of the subfamily Vaccinioideae, which also includes cranberries (the subspecies *oxycoccus*) and lingonberries (*Vaccinium vitis-idaea*). Lingonberries, prized in Scandinavia, are called partridge-berries in Newfoundland, where they are food for ptarmigan (known locally as 'partridge'), and are equally appreciated by human foragers as the basis for delicious syrups, jams, cakes and beverages. The delicate creeping snowberries (*Gaultheria hispidula*), with their tiny white fruits, described by Samuel de Champlain (1567–1635) on his journeys in New France as having the taste and texture of bananas,[22] and the wintergreen-flavoured checkerberries or teaberries (*G. procumbens*), are also members of this group. On the northwest coast of America, salal (*G. shallon*), another relative, has been gathered for millennia by Haida and other First Nations peoples. Crowberries, not just prized by crows

The 'perfect' flower of *Fragaria* x *ananassa*.

Mulberries (*Morus alba*).

Mary Delany, 'Black Whortle or Bilberries (*Vaccinium myrtillus*)', 1776, collage of coloured papers with watercolour on black-ink background.

and whimbrels but by many northern peoples, particularly the Inuit and the Sami, are the edible members of the Ericoideae, which also includes the toxic if beautiful rhododendrons and azaleas. *Arbutus unedo*, the strawberry tree (or *el madroño* in Spain, where it features along with a bear in the coat of arms of the city of Madrid) has fruit in appearance like bright-red strawberries, but in taste somewhat like figs. It is part of the Arbutoideae clan, which also includes another bear-associated plant – *Arctostaphylos uva-ursi*, the bearberry, known in North America by the euphonious name of *kinnikinnick*; the dried leaves formed part of a traditional smoking mixture used by Indigenous peoples. The *manzanita*, or little apple, is another name for members of the *Arctostaphylos* genus, found in the high chaparral country of the American Southwest and into British Columbia.

Blueberries and cranberries are archetypical berries in the popular imagination, but there are a number of true berries among the Ericales that do not necessarily spring to mind when one thinks of tiny sweet fruits, though both are widely cultivated and much relished from Asia to the Americas. The sapodilla (*Manilkara zapota*) – called naseberry in Jamaica from *néspera*, the Spanish word for 'medlar' which the fruit superficially resembles – is also a true berry with delicious orange flesh. The Chinese gooseberry family, the Actinidiaceae, is the home of *Actinidia deliciosa*, a woody vine native to China, where its fuzzy, brown berries are known colloquially as monkey peach, but are now much better known by their New Zealand moniker as kiwifruits. While kiwifruits may be called gooseberries, the true gooseberry and its congener the currant are members of an entirely different order. It is hard to think of bushy currants and prickly gooseberries sharing an ancestor with sedums and stonecrops, but all belong to the Saxifragales. There are about 160 species of the genus *Ribes*, the only species in the Grossulariaceae family, and to which both currants, red and black, and gooseberries belong. If the berry has prickles, it tends to be called a gooseberry, and if smooth, a currant. These are the fruits of temperate climates, and the *Ribes* are native to North America, South America along the spine of the Andes, Europe and Asia. The

British developed a culture of gooseberry gigantism (to be explored later) and also a taste for a 'brisk' gooseberry wine, likened to champagne by one extoller of its virtues. Elderberries, the fruit of yet another member of the broad asterid group, also serve as the basis for wines and cordials, and the flowers yield an elderflower 'champagne'. The elders (*Sambucus* sp.) and their cousins the viburnums have long provided food for people, birds and beasts, despite their toxicity. In the elders, everything but the flowers and the ripe fruit (minus the seeds) is toxic, while in the American cranberry bush (*Viburnum trilobum*), consuming large quantities of fruit can lead to unpleasant gastric symptoms. These two berry-bearing shrubs share their order (Dipsacales) with the honeysuckle family, a recent arrival in the edible berry market. Haskap berries, named after the Ainu word for the bright-blue, strangely shaped berries, are now cultivated in North America and extolled as a 'fruiticeutical', promoted as long 'known by the ancient Japanese as, "The fruit of Life longevity and Fruit of vision"'.[23]

Arbutus unedo fruit, close-up.

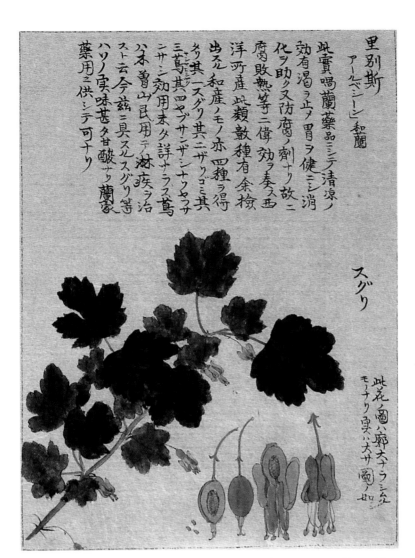

Suguri (a currant, *Ribes* species), 19th century, watercolour, from a Japanese album of fruit and fungi.

The Devil's Berries

Cousin to the Ericales are the Solanales, a number of whose members bear more recognizably berrylike fruits that have become staples in world food culture. The tomato (*Solanum* sp.) originated in South America, was imported to Europe by the end of the fifteenth century and – along with its other New World cousin the pepper (*Capsicum* sp.), whose fruit is a hollow berry (though rarely thought of as such by most consumers) – transformed Mediterranean cuisine. Tomatoes grow not only on bushes but on trees. The *tomate de árbol* or *tomaríllo* (*Solanum betaceum*) originated in the Andes, and in Ecuador is a key ingredient of the ubiquitous local hot sauce known as *ají*. It is now grown almost worldwide in Africa, India, Nepal, China, Australia and New Zealand. In Australia, another *Solanum* – *S. aviculare* – also grows on trees, or at least tall shrubs, and is known colloquially as the Kangaroo Apple. Australians also consume a number of 'bush tomatoes', some of which, like the desert raisin or *kutjera* (*S. centrale*), have been gathered for millennia by Aboriginal harvesters. Eating the berries of solanums comes with a caveat. With more than 1,300 species, *Solanum* is the largest genus in the Solanaceae or Nightshade family. The tribe also includes eggplants (aubergine), potatoes (which produce a small green and toxic berry), Cape gooseberries (*Physalis peruviana*, or goldenberry) and their relative, the non-edible but highly decorative Chinese lantern plant (*P. alkekengi*, known in French as the charming 'love in a cage' – *amours en cage*).[24] For many years after their early introduction to European gardens, however, both tomatoes and aubergines in particular were shunned.[25] People associated them with another plant in the Nightshade family – belladonna (*Atropa belladonna*), or the devil's berries – whose sweet black fruits were said to be favourites of witches. Deadly nightshade is one of the most toxic plants found in Europe and Central Asia. Naturalized in North America, it resembles its slightly less poisonous cousins, black nightshade (*Solanum nigrum*), bittersweet (*S. dulcamara*) and Jerusalem or winter cherry (*S. pseudocapsicum*). All bear attractive, brightly coloured

Chinese lantern or winter cherry (*Physalis alkekengi*) in the medicinal garden of the Royal College of Physicians, London.

berries, and Victorian doctors recounted the fatal consequences of eating them to city-dwelling children who, unlike their country cousins, did not learn to discern the deadly from the edible at their mother's knee:

> Country people generally early learn to distinguish the noxious from the innoxious, children gaining this knowledge traditionally as soon as they begin to toddle and prattle. It is not so, however, with many town-bred children, and even adults, whose idea of fruit is limited to that offered in the streets and shops for eating. They know nothing of the existence of fruit that is not good to eat, and, on their rare visits to the country, take whatever comes to hand, sometimes with disastrous consequences to themselves.[26]

As more and more children grew up distant from the countryside, the Boy Scouts, whose motto was 'Be Prepared', took measures to

Fruits of *Atropa belladonna*, Botanical Garden of Charles University, Prague, Czech Republic.

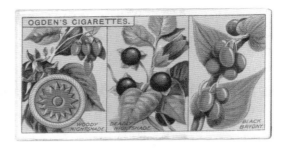

ensure the safety of members who roved country lanes. In the 1920s,
Ogden's Cigarettes, a branch of the Imperial Tobacco Company,
equipped scouts with a handy collectible cigarette card showing common poisonous berries.[27] Today Boy and Girl Scouts are taught the
handy mnemonic, 'White and yellow, kill a fellow. Purple and blue,
good for you. Red . . . could be good, could be dead.'[28] Death by berry
could, of course, be deliberate; Agatha Christie's redoubtable Miss
Marple identifies belladonna as the agent used by the murderer to
make his wife appear mad in *A Caribbean Mystery* (1964).

The solanums are not the only plants whose berries might prove
deadly in the hands of a villain. The trinity of Christmas plants – holly,
ivy and mistletoe – all bear poisonous berries, as do fragrant lily of
the valley; pokeweed (*Phytolacca americana*), whose black clusters are
sometimes mistaken for grape; the aptly named baneberry (or doll's
eyes, *Actaea* sp.) and the decorative American bittersweet (*Celastrus
scandens*). Bryony (*Bryonia* sp.), a relative of cucumbers and squashes,
is another vine with decorative but poisonous berries. The yew,
sacred to Druids, and the chinaberry (*Melia azedarach*) are widely
planted as ornamentals, and while the flesh of their bright berries is
not toxic, the seeds within are. Birds eat the fruits with abandon,
however, discarding the seeds (and fulfilling the plant's dispersal
mission). Juniper berries flavour gin, but some of the junipers
(*Juniperus sabina*) bear poison fruit. One should also not eat the unripe
fruits of mulberries or elderberries, and avoid the dark, berrylike
drupes of the buckthorns (*Rhamnus cathartica*, or purging buckthorn
– the name says it all).

Toxicity is a characteristic of many plants. Just as conspicuousness and delectability ensure that fruits are widely distributed, phyto-toxins protect the plant from overharvesting by insects and greedy frugivores. Thankfully, the multitude of edible berries beggars the imagination. Those we choose to prize and eat are embedded not just within our gustatory preferences, but deep within our cultural imaginations.

two

Berries in Mind

🪷

The value of these wild fruits is not in the mere possession or eating of them, but in the sight and enjoyment of them. The very derivation of the word 'fruit' would suggest this. It is from the Latin *fructus*, meaning 'that which is *used* or *enjoyed*.' If it were not so, then going a-berrying and going to market would be nearly synonymous experiences. Of course, it is the spirit in which you do a thing which makes it interesting, whether it is sweeping a room or pulling turnips. Peaches are unquestionably a very beautiful and palatable fruit, but the gathering of them for the market is not nearly so interesting to the imaginations of men as the gathering of huckleberries for your own use.

HENRY DAVID THOREAU, *Wild Fruits*

Berries are paradoxical – free for the picking but hard won; delicious freshly picked but once plucked, easily spoilt. They are hardy and often invasive but just as often resist cultivation. While evidence from archaeological sites and their ubiquity in folklore and language testify to their long history of consumption and use, berries were not only toilsome to gather, protected by thorns or growing low and hidden, but equally difficult to transport, their fruits too juicy and too fragile. Sometimes the berries ripen late, sometimes early. Some years there is a bumper crop, while in others they are a scarce resource. You must go where the berries are and gather them when they are ready. They were, until very recently, the very essence of the spirit of place, their harvest, as Thoreau noted, more than just a physical experience, but stimulation to the human imagination.

In Arcadia

If the berry, that luscious example of coevolution, was not exactly the manna of the classical world, it was close. In the biblical story of creation, God called the fruits of the earth from the ground on the third day. According to the Roman poet Ovid, Orpheus sang the vegetable world into being:

> When here the heaven-descended bard sat down and smote his sounding lyre, shade came to the place. There came the Chaonian oak . . . the ilex-tree bending with acorns . . . the slender tamarisk, the double-hued myrtle, the viburnum with its dark-blue berries. You also, pliant-footed ivy, came, and along with you tendrilled grapes, and the elm-trees, draped with vines; the mountain-ash, the forest-pines, the arbute-tree, loaded with ruddy fruit . . .[1]

This was the Golden Age under Time (*Kronos*), when people neither ploughed nor sowed but lived guilelessly from the fruitful earth. In *Metamorphoses*, written at the beginning of the first century of the current era, Ovid enlarged on creation stories recorded eight centuries earlier by the Greek poet Hesiod. *Metamorphoses* was much admired in the Middle Ages and the Renaissance, and fixed in the minds of many Europeans a vision of a bountiful paradise that flowed with rivers of milk and honey, and berries:

> Golden was that first age . . . The earth herself, without compulsion, untouched by hoe or plowshare, of herself gave all things needful. And men, content with food which came with no one's seeking, gathered the arbute fruit, strawberries

Cunradus
Schlapperitzi,
full-page
miniature of God
creating flowers
and plants, 1445.

from the mountain-sides, cornel-cherries, berries hanging
thick upon the prickly bramble, and acorns fallen from the
spreading tree of Jove . . .[2]

The people who dined upon these sweet gifts were themselves
free of the vices and desires of their less-perfect descendants –
they did not make war, they did not wander far from home or sail
the seven seas, nor did they demand more than their share. They
were not, however, immune to carnal desire, and in this too, berries
played their part. According to Lucretius, Ovid's near contemporary, who some fifty years later wrote *On the Nature of the Universe*,
this 'flowering infancy of the world' was also an age of free love, at
least for men:

Lucas Cranach the Elder, *The Golden Age*, c. 1530, oil on panel.

And Venus joined the bodies of lovers in the woods; for
either the woman was attracted by mutual desire, or caught
by the man's violent force and vehement lust, or by a bribe
– acorns and arbute-berries or choice pears.[3]

Berries were thus early associated in Western thought with two
sometimes conflicting notions: innocence and desire.

Innocence

Berries grew without tilling and, unlike grains or flesh, required
no transformation to make them edible and delectable. They were
indeed food of the gods, particularly suitable to innocents, like children, primitive peoples who lived in antique manner close to nature
or virtuous simple folk, who by dint of poverty relied on what nature
freely provided. In Europe, berries were early associated with the very
young. Little children were traditionally sent out strawberry picking on St John's Day, 24 June, and in some areas, where the fruit was

DEVISES

Latet anguis in herba.

deemed sacred to the Virgin Mary, they picked under the protection of the Virgin herself. Mary's company was a good thing, since evil lurked among the fragrant berries. In his Third Eclogue, the Roman poet Virgil had warned of the 'chill snake' hidden among strawberry leaves, and by the Middle Ages, the snake of Eden twined about a strawberry plant had become an emblem of corruption. Children must be aided to resist the Devil and all his works, hidden even in innocent pleasures.

Strawberries embodied other hazards for their youthful gatherers. Just as the berries were fragile and ephemeral, so were the children

Thomas Watson, after Sir Joshua Reynolds, *The Strawberry Girl*, 1774, mezzotint.

who plucked them. In Germany, strawberries symbolized children who had died young and ascended to heaven, hidden within a strawberry (whether flower or fruit is unclear). Bereft mothers forbore to eat strawberries on St John's Day for fear of inadvertently depriving their lost little ones of the strawberries they would eat in paradise, or worse – devouring their own child. (Perhaps these tales inspired the British artist Cicely Mary Barker to assign the letter 'S' in *A Flower Fairy Alphabet* to Strawberry, depicted as a winsome child in a 'party suit / Of red and white'.[4]) Blackberrying was also considered the domain of children, to which testify innumerable nineteenth-century paintings and prints of girls and boys plucking blackberries from hedgerows and hillsides. Books for children extolled the pleasures of gathering the wild fruit:

> There is nothing, I think, that children enjoy much more than blackberry gathering; and no wonder! To be in pleasant fields and woods, scrambling up and down banks, filling your baskets with the pretty bright berries, and eating a good many at the same time – all this is very delightful indeed. And if you do tear your clothes a little, and scratch and stain your hands very much, – well, it is only considered part of the fun.[5]

But children were warned never to pick the dark fruits after Michaelmas Eve in autumn, when the Devil (or in Ireland, the mischievous Pooka) was reputed to spit or even urinate on the blackberries, rendering them inedible.[6] Like strawberries, blackberries also had more sinister associations. Innumerable tragic fairy tales, from the Brothers Grimm's 'Hansel and Gretel' to the Russian tale of 'Little Snow Girl', begin when sweet youngsters are sent into

Winslow Homer, *Gathering Wild Blackberries*, 1880, wood engraving.

the deep, dark woods to pick berries. The most tragic is undoubtedly the story of the poor lost 'Babes in the Woods'. First published as a broadside ballad in 1595, the popular tale of innocence betrayed was reworked many times from the seventeenth to the nineteenth century, with a celebrated illustrated version by Randolph Caldecott in 1879. A conniving uncle seeks the death of his young nephew and niece, heirs to a fortune. After trials and tribulations, they are left to wander alone in the dark woods, where, despite the sustenance of a few hard-won berries, they perish:

> Their prettye lippes with blackberries
> Were all besmear'd and dyed;
> And when they sawe the darksome night,
> They sat them downe and cryed.

In the morning, the red-breasted robins come to cover the tiny corpses with strawberry leaves – the little children's shroud.[7]

Bilberries (a European species of blueberry) were also the harvest of children, often the rural poor, for whom, despite the idyllic pictures of Victorian poets, the berries were part of a subsistence diet:

> Come ! will you not go where the bilberries grow,
> On their beautiful bushes of green;
> Whose ruby bells smiled, in the desolate wild,
> On the far away, moorland scene?
> We are up and away, at the dawn of the day,
> Young cottagers moving in scores;
> Ere the dawn of the day we are up and away –
> Away to the bilberry moors.[8]

In America, however, the bilberry was more than simple sustenance. According to that keen enthusiast of wild fruits, Henry David Thoreau, its virtues sustained the nation. Thoreau was a passionate advocate of the wild fruits of the land, not only for their delectability but for their moral worth. He prepared an unpublished lecture on the huckleberry, which is an unabashed paean to the humble berry.[9] The huckleberry and its close cousin the blueberry were, he felt, the quintessential fruits of America (as Huckleberry Finn was, in many ways, the archetypal American), growing 'wild all over the country – wholesome, bountiful and free, a real ambrosia'.[10] And the gathering of this native bounty was more than just child's play:

> I well remember with what a sense of freedom and spirit of adventure I used to take my way across the fields with my pail, some years later, toward some distant hill or swamp, when dismissed for all day, and I would not now exchange such an expansion of all my being for all the learning in the world. Liberation and enlargement – such is the fruit which all culture aims to secure.[11]

Thoreau claimed that it was in the huckleberry fields where he served his apprenticeship and did 'considerable journeywork', and where he received 'the best schooling that I got': '*There* was the university itself, where you could learn the everlasting Laws and Medicine and Theology'.[12] He believed as well that there was something in going a-berrying that was essential to the particular genius of American life. Native fruits fed the imagination in a way that imported fruits of foreign lands could never do. He disdains the pineapple and the orange not for their taste but for their inherent value:

> Do not think, then, that the fruits of New England are mean and insignificant while those of some foreign land are noble and memorable. Our own, whatever they may be, are far more important to us than any others can be. They educate us and fit us to live here. Better for us is the wild strawberry than the pine-apple, the wild apple than the orange, the

Overleaf: Wild blueberry fields in the autumn near Parrsboro, Nova Scotia, Canada.

chestnut and pignut than the cocoa-nut and almond, and not on account of their flavor merely, but the part they play in our education.[13]

He despaired that fields were being privatized, the berries 'enslaved' and children and families turned away, 'for at the same time that we exclude mankind from gathering berries in our field, we exclude them from gathering health and happiness and inspiration and a hundred other far finer and nobler fruits than berries'.[14] For Thoreau, native fruits not only offered an opportunity to educate and inculcate moral values in those who gathered them, but they were the bread and wine of a new sacrament:

> Man at length stands in such a relation to Nature as the animals which pluck and eat as they go. The fields and hills are a table constantly spread. Diet drinks, cordials, wines of all kinds and qualities are bottled up in the skins of countless berries for the refreshment of animals, and they quaff them at every turn. They seem offered to us not so much for food as for sociality, inviting us to picnic with Nature. We pluck and eat in remembrance of her. It is a sort of sacrament, a communion – the *not* forbidden fruits, which no serpent tempts us to eat. Slight and innocent savors which relate us to nature, make us her guests, and entitle us to her regard and protection.[15]

Subsisting on 'innocent savors' of fruits and berries was also the privilege of the new Arcadians, those peoples who lived close to primeval nature on the margins of empire, in the inaccessible lands of the north or across the ocean in a New World. Classical literature abounds in examples of such 'simple' delights. In his *Natural History*, Pliny the Elder, referencing the historian Herodotus, describes the Arimphaei, a race akin to the Hyperboreans, the blessed folk who dwell in the calm at the back of the North Wind. The Arimphaei

made their homes in groves along the river Carambucis (which commentators identify with the Dvina that falls into the White Sea near
Arkhangelsk), subsisting on wild berries in an icy Arcadia.[16] Laplanders, who Thoreau described as living in 'that twilight region where
you would not expect that the sun had power enough to paint a
strawberry red' were, however, equally blessed with an abundance
of fragrant fruits, 'whose profusion is such that they stain the hoofs
of the reindeer, and the sledge of the traveller'.[17] But this was as
nothing compared to the fields of wild berries that greeted early
European settlers in the New World: 'I will end therefore with the
soyle, which is excellent so that we cannot sett downe a foot, but
tread on Strawberries, raspires, fallen mulberrie vines, acchorns,
walnutts, saxafras &c.'[18]

Such abundance encouraged writers to see the lost Arcadia in the
wilds of America. To Thoreau, the strawberries in particular were
'the first blush of a country, its morning red, a sort of ambrosial food
which grows only on Olympian soil.'[19] The travelling botanist
William Bartram described the fields of wild strawberries that dyed
the legs and feet of his horses as he journeyed through the American
southeast, prompting an Elysian rapture. Riding through Cherokee
country in 1776, he

> enjoyed a most enchanting view; a vast expanse of green
> meadows and strawberry fields; a meandering river gliding
> through, saluting in its various turnings the swelling, green,
> turfy knolls, embellished with parterres of flowers and fruit-
> ful strawberry beds; flocks of turkies strolling about them;
> herds of deer prancing in the meads or bounding over the
> hills; companies of young, innocent Cherokee virgins, some
> busy gathering the rich fragrant fruit, others having already
> filled their baskets, lay reclined under the shade of floriferous
> and fragrant native bowers of Magnolia, Azalea Philadelphus,
> perfumed Calycanthus, sweet Yellow Jessamine and cerulean
> Glycine frutescens, disclosing their beauties to the fluttering

breeze, and bathing their limbs in the cool fleeting streams;
whilst other parties more gay and libertine, were yet col-
lecting strawberries, or wantonly chasing their companions,
tantalising them, staining their lips and cheeks with the rich
fruit.[20]

It is hard to imagine a more idyllic scene, or one more inspired by the
memory of a Golden Age. But even in this New World, the primor-
dial strawberry fields were being pushed further and further away
by the march of civilization. Where once strawberries carpeted the
meadows of New Hampshire, Thoreau lamented that already in his
day, those who seek the red fruit must travel 'to the cool banks of the
North' or 'to the prairies of the Assineboin, where by its abundance
it is said to tinge the feet of the prairie horses and the buffaloes'.[21]

If Arcadia is overwhelmed by the advance of cultivation, an echo
of the idyll continues to sound in the lives of those who choose a
simple country life. That fabled rustic couple Baucis and Philemon,
despite their somewhat pinched circumstances, laid out a feast fit for
the gods for unexpected visitors:

she placed on the board some olives, green and ripe, truthful
Minerva's berries, and some autumnal cornel-cherries pickled
in the lees of wine; endives and radishes, cream cheese and
eggs, lightly roasted in the warm ashes, all served in earthen
dishes . . . Here were nuts and figs, with dried dates, plums
and fragrant apples in broad baskets, and purple grapes just
picked from the vines; in the centre of the table was a comb
of clear white honey.[22]

Their visitors were indeed gods, who drowned the more sinful inhabitants of the spoiled earth, but saved the elderly couple in reward
for their simplicity and generosity. Baucis and Philemon are classical precursors of what Thoreau called 'huckleberry people', the new
heathens:

European cornel or Cornelian cherry (*Cornus mas*).

As in old times they who dwelt on the heath, remote from towns, being backward to adopt the doctrines which prevailed in towns, were called heathen in a bad sense, so I trust that we dwellers in the huckleberry pastures, which are our heath-lands, shall be slow to adopt the notions of large towns and cities, though perchance we may be nicknamed 'huckleberry people'.

Far from the temptations of corrupt civilization, they dwell closer to the earth, living 'like birds' on the wealth of fruits 'still covering our hills as when the red men lived here':

Every bush and bramble bears its fruit. The very sides of the road are a fruit garden. The earth there teems with blackberries, huckleberries, thimbleberries, fresh and abundant – no signs of drought nor of pickers. Great shining black berries peep out at me from under the leaves upon the rocks.

This 'upcountry Eden' is 'a land flowing with milk and huckleberries'.[23] But huckleberry people were often as poor as they were virtuous. In 'Blueberries', the American poet Robert Frost described the Lorens, that thrifty country family he encountered on the road, as being brought up 'on wild berries, they say, / Like birds.' It was, he acknowledged, 'a nice way to live, / Just taking what Nature is willing to give, / Not forcing her hand with harrow and plow.'[24] It was the fabled life of dream when all nature spoke and we heeded that another earlier American poet, Ralph Waldo Emerson, heard as he plucked the wise berries from their vines:

'May be true what I had heard,
Earth's a howling wilderness
Truculent with fraud and force,'
Said I, strolling through the pastures,
And along the riverside.

Caught among the blackberry vines,
Feeding on the Ethiops sweet,
Pleasant fancies overtook me:
I said, 'What influence me preferred,
Elect, to dreams thus beautiful?'
The vines replied, 'And didst thou deem
No wisdom to our berries went?'[25]

Desire

The charming Madonna who sits in a field of strawberries is known
as the 'Fruitful Virgin'. Like the Madonna, the strawberry is humble
(ground-loving) and fragrant, one of the plants in Eden's garden
before the Fall, the fruit of the spirit and an emblem of righteousness.
But the strawberry is also the fruit of Venus – ruby red, heart-shaped,
an aphrodisiac with heady scent and fugitive sweetness, and despite
its apparent purity, seductive. Edmund Spenser, he of *The Faerie
Queene*, wrote of his lover that 'Comming to kisse her lyps, (such
grace I found) / Me seem'd I smelt a gardin of sweet flowres'. Her lips
were like gillyflowers, her cheeks like roses, but 'Her goodly bosome
lyke a Strawberry bed'.[26] Strawberries are a gift between lovers and
an inducement to marriage, as generations of children learned from
the nursery rhyme:

Curly locks! curly locks! wilt thou be mine?
Thou shalt not wash dishes, nor yet feed the swine;
But sit on a cushion and sow a fine seam,
And feed upon strawberries, sugar, and cream![27]

Among the Cherokee, they are just the thing to heal a lovers' spat.
The first man and first woman lived together happily, for a time.
Then they began to quarrel and the woman left her husband, walking
east to the Sun lands. Her distressed husband followed, but his wife
would not look back. The Sun took pity on the husband and attempted

Anonymous, after monogrammist PW of Cologne, 'St Anne with Virgin and Child', from a Flemish prayer book, 1500–1520.

to stop the woman in her tracks by tempting her with the finest fruits of the land. First, ripe huckleberries sprung up along her path, but she did not stop. Then luscious blackberries, but she did not slow down. Red serviceberries, the fruit of the Amelanchier, appeared, but she did not taste them. Then she came to a patch of strawberries.

Porcelain cream-jug with applied strawberries and leaves in high relief,
Chelsea Porcelain Factory, London, 1745–8.

She stopped, she ate a few, and her desire for her husband returned.
She gathered the ripe red berries and returned to share them with
her husband, who was coming along the path to meet her.[28] As Dr
William Butler mused in seventeenth-century England, 'Doubtless
God could have made a better berry, but doubtless God never did.'[29]

But strawberries, of course, have a darker side. They also symbolize the wanton woman, the seductress hiding beneath the innocent white flower, and the dangers of romantic passion. Shakespeare 'spotted' Desdemona's lost handkerchief with strawberries, symbols both of purity and of the adulteress.[30] Othello, unfortunately, saw the strawberry in its darkest light, and Desdemona's tragic fate was sealed. Strawberries may carpet the fields of paradise, but beware the snake in the grass.

Is this the message in *The Garden of Earthly Delights* by the fifteenth-century Dutch artist Hieronymus Bosch, more properly known by its original title, the 'painting of the strawberry' (*el quadro del madroño*)? In the central panel of a triptych, created one presumes for the altar of a chapel, naked men and women preen, cavort, caress and bathe in a fantastical garden replete not only with the biggest, juiciest strawberries imaginable, but with huge bunches of glistening grapes and enormous pomegranates. There are also sprays of gigantic black and red currants hoisted like banners, pink gooseberries, mulberries carried like purses, blackberries the size of a man's head and cherries big enough to be worn as fanciful diadems by charming ladies who wear nothing else. And there is the fruit of the arbutus or strawberry tree, the *madroño* of the title, being plucked by eager hands or offered up by giant birds. The arbute-berry was, of course, the favoured fruit of the lascivious Golden Age, and to contemporary viewers at the court of Philip II, both strawberry and *madroño* had salacious associations. Strawberries were symbols of lust and unchaste women, and the *madroño* was the fruit of drunkenness.[31] When left too long on the tree, the berries fermented, and tempted not only human revellers but bears. Bosch includes a bear climbing an arbutus tree on the left-hand panel of his triptych, an image familiar to Spaniards since the thirteenth century from the coat of arms of the city of Madrid.

What is the meaning of this riotous berrying of the naked masses? In 1605 the librarian at El Escorial, Fray José de Sigüenza, saw the grotesque strawberries and arbute-berries as embodiments of the

Hieronymus Bosch, *The Garden of Earthly Delights*, 1490–1500,
oil on panel, triptych, detail.

ephemeral nature of earthly passion, which like 'the passing taste of
strawberries or the strawberry plant and its pleasant odor, they are
hardly remembered once it has passed'.[32] Others saw a prelapsarian
fable – an evocation of the cavorting and feasting of a Golden Age,
what the world might have been like if Eve had not been tempted
by the chill serpent of Eden. Or perhaps the artist had in mind a
depiction of the sinful ways of men and women in the postlapsarian
world before the Great Flood. Monstrous fruits and animals were
the products of fertile soil, and the most fertile ground imaginable to
medieval commentators on the Bible was found on earth before the
Great Flood. After forty days and forty nights of rain, however, the
wondrous fruits of the earth on which men and women had subsisted
were swept away, and unlike those dwellers in paradise or Arcadia,
Noah and his heirs were forced to become meat-eaters.

Strawberries, whether on the ground or in trees, are not the only
berries appreciated by lovers – tragic or happy. The mulberry seems
an emblem of thwarted love. Its berries turned from white to red with

Hieronymus Bosch, *The Garden of Earthly Delights*, 1490–1500,
oil on panel, triptych, centre panel.

the blood of the ill-fated Pyramus and Thisbe, precursors to Romeo
and Juliet who, mistaken in each other's fate, kill themselves beneath
the mulberry tree. In the traditional ballad, 'The True-lover's Trip
to the Strawberry Beds', the lovers disport themselves in the shade
of a mulberry tree:

> On the Strawberry banks all so pleasant and gay,
> There blessed with true-love, I spent a short day
> Where the sun shed his rays thro' the mulberry tree,
> And the streams formed a mirror for my true love and me.

Isaac Cruikshank, *The Mulberry-tree*, illustration to a popular song
lamenting the vagaries of life, 1808.

But their pleasure is short, for the young man is taken to be a sol-
dier and the singer goes no more to the strawberry fields.[33] In Victor
Hugo's celebrated poem 'Vieille chanson du jeune temps' (An Old
Song of Youth), a callow boy watches as the lovely Rose stretches her
pale arms to pluck mulberries:

> *Rose, droite sur ses hanches,*
> *Leva son beau bras tremblant*
> *Pour prendre une mûre aux branches*
> *Je ne vis pas son bras blanc.*[34]

Blind to her beauty and *la nature amoureuse*, only in retrospect does the poet regret the lost opportunity for love that haunts him still.

Berry picking, of course, is a good opportunity for dalliance. The strawberry fields are the scene of love and betrayal in Ingmar Bergman's classic film *Smultronstället* (Wild Strawberries, 1957). It is while picking the innocent strawberries that the protagonist loses his sweetheart to his brother. In the traditional Scottish ballad 'The Blaeberry Courtship', the eager suitor praises the charms of picking blaeberries, or blueberries – the symbol of the remote Highlands – to woo his somewhat reluctant Lowland love:

> Will you go to the Highlands, my jewel, with me?
> Will you go to the Highlands, the flocks for to see?
> It is healthy, my dear jewel, to breathe the sweet air,
> And to pull the blaeberries in the forest so fair.[35]

In Ireland, bilberries were the fruits of courtship. On Bilberry Sunday in August (linked to the ancient harvest festival of Lughnasa), young lads and girls would climb the hills in search of deep-blue berries, to be made into bracelets by the boys or baked into cakes by the girls as gifts for sweethearts. Strangely, the other berry love token of Ireland hangs on a strawberry-tree. Called in Irish the *Caíthne*, isolated groves of the Mediterranean arbutus grow in Killarney, remnants of a forest that once stretched across the ancient land bridge from Brittany. Red-barked, with white flowers, its dark leaves evergreen, it is a symbol of steadfast love:

> My love's an arbutus
> By the borders of Lene,
> So slender and shapely
> In her girdle of green . . .
>
> Alas, fruit and blossom
> Shall lie dead on the lea,

And Time's jealous fingers
Dim your young charms, Machree.
But unranging, unchanging,
You'll still cling to me,
Like the evergreen leaf
To the arbutus tree.[36]

But it is the blackberry or bramble that specially twines around lovers' hearts. In the traditional Irish ballad 'Bláth na Sméar', the beloved is 'the white flower of the blackberry, she's the sweet flower of the raspberry, she's the best herb in excellence for the sight of the eyes.'[37] In France, it is the dark panther of love that is surrounded by a thicket of blackberries. Like the bramble, love can wound, but sweet fruit is the reward.

Blackberries, or brambles, are associated with other kinds of desire, both sacred and profane. Biblical scholars thought that the burning bush from which God spoke to Moses may have been a bramble, since there is, in fact, a very long-lived bramble native to the Middle East (*Rubus ulmifolius* subsp. *sanctus*), a specimen of which is revered at St Catherine's Monastery in Sinai as a descendant of this first flaming bush. The blackberry's prickly branches may have been woven into the Crown of Thorns, though that honour has also gone to holly, the red berries stained with the blood of Christ. Being so black, however, the bramble is also reputed to be the fruit of the Devil (who spoils the berries at Michaelmas) and in the language of flowers, it stands for lowliness, envy and remorse. Its less savoury reputation may stem from one of the earliest parables in the Old Testament – the king of the trees: 'The trees went forth on a time to anoint a king over them; and they said unto the olive tree, Reign thou over us.' The olive refused, as did the fig and the grape, all preferring their useful roles as providers of food and cheer. But the bramble accepted with an alarming ultimatum: 'If in truth ye anoint me king over you, then come and put your trust in my shadow: and if not, let fire come out of the bramble, and devour the cedars of Lebanon'

Arthur Rackham, *The Fir-tree and the Bramble*, 1912, illustration. Aesop's fable upends the biblical story and praises the humble berry-rich bramble over the arrogant fir.

(Judges 9:7–15). The lowly bramble could claim no use except as shade, and so leapt at the chance of preferment, threatening fire (and perhaps brimstone) on the great trees if they refused. Surely this was evidence of vegetable evil. Blackberries would even betray their most ardent fans. Seamus Heaney, the Irish poet, in his 'Blackberry-picking', describes his childhood lust for the sweet fruit, rushing to the fields when the berries ripened. Torn by thorns, he hoarded his hard-won berries, only to find his glistening treasure quickly fermented, soured, rotted. Like strawberries, the blackberries hid a sharp-toothed adder: time.

Surely the darkest and most evil tale of the blackberry is the tale of Lubelle. The story told around the fire to the pickers in the cotton fields of the American South began, 'Once there was a little girl named Lubelle who liked to play with snakes.' Lubelle's room was 'dirty, dirty, dirty'. One day, her mother tired of the mess and started to clean her daughter's very dirty room. She cleaned the windows to let in the light, she brushed the cobwebs, threw out piles of bones and burned the filthy sheets, but when she came to the closet, Lubelle tried to pull her back. Inside the closet her mother found a huge black snake, 'that long low devil'. She chopped off its head with a cotton hoe and that was when Lubelle began to pine. She pined so much that despite her mother's care, she died:

> And after they wrapped her in her winding sheet, they buried her in a watery grave next to the coal black snake. And today, in the spot where they both rest, you will find a black-berry vine. They say she is the berries and the snake is the stickers. And if you want to get a Lubelle berry, I say if you want to eat a berry, if you want to taste a Lubelle berry, you got to go through the snake.[38]

From darkness to earthiness, but far from saintly, is the humble gooseberry. 'Old Gooseberry' is another name for that 'long low Devil', Satan. It is Satan who leads man into temptation, particularly when 'gooseberries' is slang for testicles and 'gooseberry pudding' for a woman. Perhaps that is why babies were said to be found under a gooseberry bush, or why foolish antics were the occupation of a 'gooseberry fool'. In contrast, elder is never foolish and has a powerful charm; a handful of elderberries will hold off the Devil on *Berchtentag* or 'Bertha Night' (as the Feast of the Epiphany was called in Austria and Germany), when he is particularly evil. But then all berries have their charm to those who seek them out, either for feast or fortune.

three
Berries in the Hand
🪷

Traditional life is hard work . . .

MARY LOCKWOOD, 'TUNDRA GATHERING'

I f you were to judge berry picking based on the descriptions or images of nineteenth-century writers and painters, you would assume it to be child's play:

> One of the prettiest sights that greets one's eye in the districts where it abounds, is that of a party of rustic children 'a-bilberrying' (for the greater portion of those that come to market are collected by children); there they may be seen, knee deep in the 'wires,' or clambering over the broken gray rocks to some rich nest of berries, their tanned faces glowing with health, and their picturesque dress (or undress) – with here and there bits of bright red, blue, or white – to the painter's eye contrasting beautifully with the purple, gray and brown of the moorland, and forming all together rich pictorial subjects.[1]

While children might enjoy a day in the fields or woods picking and eating as they went, for many, the berry harvest was more than diversion. In traditional societies, berries were and are an essential part of people's diet, and berry picking shapes the annual round for women, children and whole communities.

Gathering

Among North American Indigenous peoples, the berry harvest marks the calendar. The Natchez people of Mississippi called April the 'strawberry moon', and for the Abenaki of the Great Lakes, July meant 'when the blueberries are ripe'. The Yakima of the Northwest celebrate first fruits in September, the berry month. Picking was the particular work of women and younger children, and when the berries called, they went to field and forest. Saskatoon berries (service-berries), blueberries and huckleberries, gooseberries and currants, blackberries, raspberries, strawberries, cloudberries, salal berries, crow-berries and cranberries – all were and are relished, both for their food value as well as medicinal uses. Wild fruits are good sources of ascorbic acid, as well as other nutrients and vitamins, and many berries are steeped as tea or chewed, as ingredients in traditional Indigenous pharmacopeias.[2] It is not only humans who love berries. Bears are particularly fond of them, as are birds. Among the Haida on the Northwest Coast, highbush cranberry (*Viburnum edule*) is said to be the food of Raven, the trickster. For the Iroquois, strawberries are linked to the original creation, the gift of Sky Woman along with the three sisters of traditional agriculture – corn, beans and squash. They are the first fruits of spring, celebrated each year at the annual straw-berry festival, and nurtured by the little people – the Gan-da-yah. Huckleberries are also highly valued by both Gitksan and Wet'suwet'en of the interior of British Columbia. Traditionally, they were eaten dried during the winters – they are an important source of carbohy-drates – but they were also used in trade with coastal nations, and exchanged as gifts at potlatches.[3] Henry David Thoreau documented the extensive use the Algonquin made of his beloved huckleberries, describing how they ate the fruit fresh or dried, mixed into breads and puddings, and how they gathered them for sale in their com-merce with settlers. Berries also thrive on the tundra of the far north, creating a rich tapestry of fruits for Inuit gatherers – blue *tungujut* (blueberries/bilberries), black *paungnait* (crowberries), red *kallait*

Winslow Homer, *Berry Pickers*, 1873, watercolour.

(bearberries) and *kimminnait* (mountain cranberries), and golden *aqpiit* (cloudberries/bakeapples).

Each year, women and children left for the berry patches with the tools of the trade, including small and large baskets often woven from roots or formed from birchbark, and special berry combs made of wood, or on the Northwest Coast, from salmon backbones. Mary Lockwood remembers the equipment her family carried on a berry-ing expedition in Alaska. Her mother's bucket

> was a special one made of steam-curved wood, with the seam bound by a tough walrus thong. Once bound, a carved bowl was fitted at the bottom of the frame. At the top was an ivory handle. For the rest of us, different sizes of coffee and Crisco cans were transformed into buckets by fitting wire handles through two opposite holes punched at the top of each can with a quick pound of a hammer on a number ten nail. Several strands of wire were twisted over and over to create a handle that would prevent the cutting of one's hand with the weight of berries.[4]

Klikitat berry basket, c. 1895–1905, plant fibres and hide, Columbia River Valley, south-central Washington, United States.

Marion Aasivaaryuk remembered too that in Nunavut, 'When there were lots of berries, we used to bring a skin, and then pick berries and put them on the skin, take them back to camp and ask other people to come and feast on berries.'[5] Fresh berries were delicious, but most were hauled home and preserved for winter use, often dried in the sun or over a fire, or boiled into pastes and then dried. Pemmican, the journey food of the prairies, was made by pounding dried meat and fat with berries. The acid in the berries lowers the pH, resisting bacteria and creating a long-lasting, high-energy, easily transportable food. Some tart fruits like cranberries could be kept in water-filled containers under a layer of oil, sweetening over the course of the winter. Where it was cold enough, berries could be stored in a pit dug into the ground, or simply left as they grew, frozen under the snow, to be dug out at will.[6] Inuit would sometimes ferment wild berries by placing them in a seal 'poke', or more recently, a barrel. For a special treat, they still make *akutaq*, or 'Eskimo ice cream', by whipping berries with fat and sometimes snow.[7]

Indigenous peoples not only knew where and when to seek wild berries; they also managed the productivity of their hereditary garden patches. In nineteenth-century America, relocation and resettlement

Samuel L. Thomas, Iroquois hand-bag, beaded with humming bird and strawberries, 2001. Niagara Falls, United States.

of communities disrupted traditional berry harvesting. When their territories were given over to white settlers for cultivation, Indigenous leaders fought to maintain the right to gather on the lands that had once been theirs, and that they had improved.[8] The blueberry barrens of Maine were, in fact, the creation of Indigenous gardeners, who knew that blueberries and huckleberries in particular thrive on recently burned-over lands, and that controlled burning would increase yields.[9] These traditional practices were often misunderstood by government forest services, and periodic burning was suppressed, with a subsequent decline in the productivity of the berry gardens.[10] Berrying was not only a means of physical sustenance but reinforced a social community. At times when the berries were particularly lush, or when a special patch was discovered, whole communities would decamp for the berry fields. An Ojibwe woman, Marie Livingston of Bad River, described an 'Eldorado' her father had found in Wisconsin in the early 1900s:

Pemmican ball.

Iced *akutaq* made from blueberries, raspberries and vegetable shortening.

My father had come across a patch of berries which was approximately one mile square. It had originally been part of a Jack Pine forest through which a raging fire had swept two years previous and made it a real Eldorado for berry seekers ... The berries were so large and thick that it was impossible to avoid stepping on them; the clusters looked like grapes.[11]

These community harvests did not necessarily meet the approval of the non-Indigenous authorities. A nineteenth-century American missionary complained that berrying was 'one great holy-day for the Indians'. Unsurprisingly, his congregation preferred 'to spend their summer Sundays in the meadows of "Indian Heaven" instead of listening to sermons that promised a Christian paradise'.[12] Berrying may have been hard work, but it came, as Mary Lockwood noted, with exceptional rewards, even for tired children:

we spread out farther to approximately a quarter-square mile, and picked even more of the dusky blueberries, the shiny-headed orange salmonberries and the vibrant red and black cranberries and blackberries. Random wanderings broke mechanical movement until the swagger, reach, and sway of wild harvest led one into earth's sweet embrace.[13]

Gardening

While missionaries might disapprove, the annual berry harvests were a natural resource that sustained both native and settler communities in North America. Indigenous pickers found a ready market for their harvest in the settlers, who themselves decamped for the berry fields when the fruit was ripe.[14] The burning of a pine forest outside Philadelphia in the late eighteenth century resulted in a 325-hectare (800 ac) strawberry garden, where the berries were so profuse that 'The people of the towns . . . from distances of more than 20 miles [32 km] were accustomed to gather and carry off these strawberries, in quantities almost incredible.'[15] Thoreau delighted in seeing the farmer's wife ('a masculine wide-eyed woman of the fields') spending the summer in the berry patch, her labour supplemented by children let out from school:

> The season of berrying is so far respected that the school children have a vacation then, and many little fingers are busy picking these small fruits. It is even a pastime, not a drudgery, though it often pays well beside. The First of August is to them the anniversary of Emancipation in New England.

But this idyllic state of affairs belonged to 'Young America'. 'Old America' was making much more of a business out of berry picking:

> But ah we have fallen on evil days! I hear of pickers ordered out of the huckleberry fields, and I see stakes set up with

Winslow Homer, *The Strawberry Bed*, 1868, wood engraving.

written notices forbidding any to pick them . . . What becomes of the true value of country life – what, if you must go to market for it?[16]

By the early nineteenth century, wild berry picking began to transform from subsistence gathering to commercial harvesting. The blueberry barrens of Maine were leased for harvest and each year, in imitation of Indigenous practice, the renters poured kerosene into a bent pipe with a cloth plug to serve as a wick, and torched a section of their lease, harvesting the crop the following year to provide fresh berries for the urban markets of Boston and Montreal.[17]

The first cranberries were shipped to New York from Cape Cod in 1820 and by 1840 the New England cranberry industry was in full swing, propelled by new techniques of planting and harvesting. Cranberries were shipped in barrels by boat to both American and European markets, but they also rode the rails. In 1881 New Jersey alone sent over 35,000 bushels of cranberries by train to Philadelphia.[18] Even the strawberry, that most fragile of fruits, was shipped by train.

New York, the greatest strawberry market in the world, had relied on delivery by sailing sloops or ferries, but on a June night in 1847, 80,000 baskets of strawberries arrived in New York on the 'Pea Line' train from New Jersey. By 1865 strawberry season extended from one month to four and even longer, as the trains brought boxes of berries from ever further afield. In the spring of 1888, the first shipment of Florida strawberries arrived in Manhattan by refrigerator car: 'From a beginning of six cars in 1887, sixty were operated in 1888, 600 in 1891, and over 60,000 in 1901.'[19] By the end of the nineteenth century, berry picking had changed from rural pastime to industrial occupation.

This was as true in Europe as it was in the Americas. Hawkers sold *fraises* (strawberries) on the streets of sixteenth-century Paris.[20] And if John Lidgate, who wrote the poem 'London Lickpenny', is to be believed, strawberries were being sold in the streets of London as early as 1430:

Then unto London I dyde me hye,
Of all the land it bearyeth the pryse.

Trade card of Edward Owen, fruiterer, c. 1785. Note the pottles of strawberries.

'Strawberries. All ripe! All ripe!' — The Street Fruit Trade', from *Street Life in London* (1877) by John Thomson and Adolphe Smith.

'Gode pescod,' one began to cry,
'Strabery rype, and cherrys in the ryse.'[21]

These tiny wild strawberries were sold in 'pottles', little handfuls often poured into cabbage leaves or tapering cylindrical baskets. According to Henry Mayhew, that dedicated chronicler of London life, over 1.5 million pottles of strawberries at 2d. per pottle were being sold on the streets of London in the mid-nineteenth century; they were far and away the most popular of the small fruits eaten fresh, followed only by raspberries. Half of all strawberries were sold by costermongers from their carts:

> The coster's best customers are dwellers in the suburbs, who purchase strawberries on a Sunday especially, for dessert, for they think that they get them fresher in that way than by reserving them from the Saturday night, and many

are tempted by seeing or hearing them cried in the streets. There is also a good Sunday sale about the steam-wharfs, to people going 'on the river,' especially when young women and children are members of a party . . .

Costermongers were also selling over three-quarters of the 140,000 bushels of gooseberries that arrived in the markets, mostly sold green for dumplings, 'the working-people's Sunday dessert'.[22] The challenge was in ensuring that fragile fresh fruits arrived in a condition to command the highest prices. The answer was to establish market gardens within convenient distance of the city markets. By the seventeenth century, local farmers were supplying London with fresh vegetables, and by the end of the eighteenth century, 'inquiries made in each parish' revealed that there were 'about 5,000 acres [2,000 ha], within twelve miles of the metropolis, constantly cultivated for the supply of the London markets', of which 800 [325 ha] were devoted to fruits.[23] William Cobbett noted in 1825 that the country around St Mary Cray, now a part of greater London, was 'a series of fruit gardens; cherries, or apples, or pears, or plums, above, and gooseberries, currants, raspberries or filberts beneath'.[24] In Paris,

Thomas Rowlandson (1756–1827), *Picking Mulberries*, undated, watercolour on paper.

Giovanni Vendramini, after Francis Wheatley, *Strawberries, Scarlet Strawberries*, 'The Cries of London' series, 1795, colour stipple engraving.

the French method of intensive cultivation by *maraîchiers* in raised plots (well fertilized by manure and *poudrette*[25]) was the envy of Europe. Despite the increase in population at the beginning of the nineteenth century, there were still in 1830 almost 600 hectares (1,485 ac) in Paris devoted to market gardens and orchards, and 95 per cent of the fruits and vegetables eaten in the capital were grown in the Île-de-France.[26]

Sturdier fruits like apples came to urban markets by horse and cart or by water, but much was borne on the backs of countrywomen. The celebrated peaches of Montreuil were

> carried to Paris, by the females of the village, of all ages; and these set off, in bands, by 1 or 2 o'clock in the morning; for all the wholesale markets of the capital are held at very early hours.[27]

In 1811 the market gardeners of London raised great quantities of raspberries, which they sent to the distillers in 'swing carts', but

> fruit for the table is carried in head-loads by women, who come principally from Shropshire, and the neighbourhood of Kingsdown in Wiltshire. The fruit is gathered very early in the morning, 12 women being employed to gather a load, which is 12 gallons (of three pints each,) the pay for gathering is a penny halfpenny per gallon. One of the gatherers carries the load to Covent Garden market (a distance of about 10 miles, for which she has 3s. 6d. It is needless to say that they perform but one journey in the day; the Hammersmith women perform three, and receive 8d. for each journey, over and above their day's work. At Kensington they are paid sixpence, and frequently go four times in the day. These women usually go at the rate of nearly five miles an hour.[28]

In 1834 it was estimated that more than 2,000 women were employed in carrying strawberries to London from surrounding gardens. Up before light, they picked the berries, packed them in pottles and then, sometimes running the 11 to 13 kilometres (7 or 8 mi.) with an 18-kilogram (40 lb) basket balanced on their heads, they delivered their produce to market the same morning.[29] The coming of the railways eased their loads and extended the distance fruit could travel from market gardens. As early as 1840, fruits were being distributed by train not only to London but to other major urban centres such as Liverpool and Manchester. In Hampshire, a strawberry boom began in the late 1860s after the passing of the Enclosure Act, when small plots became more readily available to aspiring farmers. Farmers needed cash crops, and the strawberry answered the need. In the parish of Titchfield, what had been 'waste heather land' was cut up 'into small allotments generally consisting of a few acres of strawberry fields round a cottage'. In season, the entire community turned to picking: 'the schools are closed, and all the children go to work in the strawberry fields'.[30] Production increased exponentially, and by the early twentieth century, the railways were laying on 'strawberry specials' to bring over 3,000 tonnes of fruit in season to Covent Garden from what had become the 'Strawberry Coast'.[31]

In France, the burgeoning railways brought into Paris not only fruits, but migrants from the country. By 1852 the city had more than 1 million residents, and the demand for housing rolled over the grounds of the older market gardens, forcing them to relocate to peripheral neighbourhoods and suburbs such as Marcoussis, and even further afield. The Syndicat des fraisiéristes de Plougastel-Daoulas

Cueillette des fraises (Picking Strawberries), Plougastel-Daoulas,
France, c. 1900, postcard.

Isaac Cruikshank, 'Folkstone Strawberries or more Carraway
Comfits for Mary Ann', 1810, hand-coloured etching.

shipped berries not only to Paris but, taking advantage of the Great
Eastern Railway, to Britain. By the early twentieth century, growers
all over France used the railways to get their products to the Paris
market still fresh and ripe. In the Val du Lot in the Cahors region,
over three hundred *fraiseuses* would descend on Caillac for the annual
strawberry harvest. In Moselle, particularly around the town of
Woippy, strawberry growing began in the 1860s, and by 1937 the
region was sending 8,000 tonnes to markets in France, Switzerland
and Germany.[32]

Cultivating

A mix of growing urban populations, new industries such as canning
and preserving and the opening of new markets for hitherto hard-
to-obtain small fruits turned berries into field crops. Women and
children, while still the principal pickers, could no longer keep
up with demand, and berries, as they do, waited for no man or
woman. When ripe, they had to be picked. Berry picking at the

industrial scale was no longer a pleasant day in the country, but hard, unforgiving and ill-paid labour:

> Up early and late – men, women, boys and little children, Community folks and village folks, riding, driving and railroading, night and day, and all about strawberries. For why? Because there are five acres [2 ha] of the crimson, juicy fruit-cones, on which sun and dew are pouring their final ripeness, and which are to be picked now or never, and got to the waiting appetites and teaspoons of our city cousins. Come on and at five in the morning we will commence.

The day that started so early in the morning often ended late at night. Not only did the berries have to be picked, they had to be packed in crates 'for the night train and boat for New York. This keeps many of our people busy till 9 or 10 o'clock.'[33] The harvest lasted only two or three weeks, and for their labours, the pickers made 'from 1 ½ to 2 ½ cents per box, at which rate some girls make 60 cents in four hours.'[34] By the 1880s in the United States, the fields of strawberries and cranberries covered thousands of acres and required hundreds of itinerant workers to pick the harvest, including former slaves. Freed from their plantations at the end of the Civil War, they were driven to seek 'work where it might be found'. Berry picking was described as

> an inviting field; the hours were short, the pay good, and the opportunity for amusement unlimited. To a great army of this floating labor, berry picking was a picnic, eagerly anticipated and enthusiastically enjoyed.[35]

While work in the open air might be preferable to the factory, the conditions under which the pickers lived in the fields were appalling. From 1908 to 1924, the photographer Lewis Hine travelled throughout the United States for the National Child Labor Committee, tramping through bogs and fields and photographing families of

Lewis Hine, 'Mrs Bissie and family. They all work in fields near Baltimore in summer and have worked at Biloxi, Miss. for two years.' Baltimore, Maryland, July 1909.

Italian immigrants from Philadelphia, Syrians from Boston, Poles and black Portuguese 'Bravas', who picked cranberries in Massachusetts, Wisconsin and New Jersey, and strawberries in Delaware, Maryland and Kentucky. He met children as young as four who helped out in the fields, five-year-olds who had been picking since they were three, and children who could not spell their names or did not know their age. He met the McNadd family on Truitt's strawberry farm at Cannon, Delaware:

> Oscar who is 7 years of age is picking berries his third season, averaging 34 quarts per day. Eve, 11 years of age, is picking berries her fifth season, averaging 100 quarts per day. Madge, 8 years old, picking berries fifth season, averaging 45 quarts per day. Alberta, 5 years old, second season, averaging 19 quarts per day . . .

They picked steadily from sun up to sun down, the girls carrying their pails and trays to the barrels or the 'bushel man'. Hine estimated the berry trays weighed between 11 and 13 kilograms (25 and 30 lb), and the cranberry boxes about 6.8 kilograms (15 lb) – 'Not a very happy job!', said ten-year-old Mary Gilbert. There were families who picked summers in the north and winters in the south, moving with the harvest like migrating birds. On the cranberry bogs this 'great army' lived in makeshift barracks:

> One was described as being 16' x 40' with a partition through the center and a chimney on the end. At each end there were two tiers of four bunks separated by matched board partitions. Each bunk was 4' wide and held two people. The men occupied one end of the structure, and the women the other. Arranged in such a fashion, the houses could hold between sixty and seventy-five men, women, and children.[36]

Lewis Hine, 'Jim Waldine, 1023 Carpenter St., Philadelphia, 6 years old, been picking cranberries two years. Also Sam Frohue, 9 years old, been picking two years, could not spell his own name. 1106 Titten St., Philadelphia. (This is the fourth week of school in Philadelphia and people will stay here two weeks more.)' Theodore Budd's Bog at Turkeytown, near Pemberton, New Jersey, September 1910.

In the strawberry fields, they would resort to disused chicken coops, one-room shacks or temporary lean-tos. The season began in May, and many children left school until the harvest ended in the autumn, missing weeks of classes. One mother, whose children picked wild blackberries in Kentucky, reasoned, 'They haint got money fer books so they have to git a little from the berryin'.'[37] Even if they berried from dawn to dusk, there was no guarantee that a picker would have money in hand by the end of the day. Pickers were paid by how much they picked, and growers devised a number of schemes to keep tallies. Newfoundland, that rocky outcrop in the North Atlantic, is strewn with blueberries. Women and children traditionally picked the berries for home canning and baking, but in the hungry 1930s, whole families went out on the barrens seeking to earn cash for the things they could not forage or make. Many were paid with a 'berry note' issued by the store to the picker, which could be redeemed for goods at the same store. The price paid per gallon varied widely and by the late 1930s, some berry pickers went on strike for better pay per gallon, only to be arrested by police called in to restore order.[38]

Russell Lee, 'Children of Indian blueberry pickers in truck', near Littlefork, Minnesota, 1937.

In Sarcoxie, Missouri, which, for a time, boasted it was the 'strawberry capital of the world' (in 1897 they hired 10,000 pickers), workers were given metal tokens with a strawberry on one side and the size of their pick on the other; these could be exchanged for goods or for cash at the bank. Tokens came in various sizes, becoming so popular among pickers that they were considered coinage; banned by the United States Treasury in the early 1900s, they were replaced by cardboard strawberry 'tickets'.[39]

Child labour was also a feature of the berry harvest in Britain. Children worked alongside itinerant groups of Gypsies and day labourers, some even being given 'picking holidays' from schools, but others simply truant. A local schoolmaster complained that,

> Out of 166 children on the Books, the Average Atten[danc]e last week was but 129 . . . This week threatens to be even worse: there are 48 children away this morning. Strawberry picking is given as the reason.

Picking was a dawn-to-dusk business and one resident of the strawberry country in Hampshire remembered that, 'Even until the Second World War, it was common to hear strawberry pickers arriving on foot from Southampton at 4.30 or 5 o'clock in the morning.'[40] The pickers walked, but the berries went to London by train. Baskets of strawberries would arrive by horse-drawn cart at the railway station in the late afternoon, where there were 'teams of small boys who had to lie on their fronts to pack the specially constructed shelves in the railway carriages with baskets of strawberries.'[41] In Scotland, the berry town of Blairgowrie drew legions of school children, travellers and casual workers to the country. In 1905, following a number of local scandals, growers worked to attract a 'respectable class of picker' to the 'delightful' countryside. They were successful, and up to 1,500 women and girls from the city came to stay in the dormitories of 'Tin City' and harvest gooseberries. Mothers would send their children for their summer holidays to pick at Blairgowrie, to earn enough to buy a

'Holiday Work – 4,000 Women Wanted', First World War poster.

school uniform and get themselves something new.[42] During wartime, schoolchildren were called to perform their patriotic duty picking berries for the war effort. School children would collect blackberries and join the land army during the holidays. For some, it was a holiday; Barbara Mason recalled her experience with pleasure, remembering that as a ten-year-old girl in 1939 she found little difficulty in picking 45 kilograms (100 lb) of raspberries in a day.[43]

Children disappeared from the cranberry bogs of New England with the invention of a heavier, more efficient cranberry scoop that could only be wielded by men, and by the 1960s mechanized cranberry harvesters made the great bog armies obsolete. Not so in the strawberry fields; the young *fraiseuses* of Caillac and the mothers of Scotland were the vanguard of thousands of women who, compelled by circumstance, continue to go annually to the strawberry fields of France, Italy, Spain and Morocco. Women are preferred because, according to one Italian grower, fragile fruits demand a delicate touch.[44] Every season since the turn of the twenty-first century, thousands of women – *Dames des fraises, doigts de fée* (Strawberry ladies, with nimble fingers) — come to Spain from Morocco to pick berries in the stifling heat of the plastic greenhouses.[45] In Morocco, since intensive strawberry cultivation began in the 1990s, 20,000 pickers, 90 per cent women, gather the small fruits.[46] Argentina's intensive strawberry cultivation employs, according to the International Labor Organization, thousands of children under the age of seventeen: 'They are specifically utilised on strawberry farms due to their small hands that don't bruise the berries, and the fact that they can easily reach the berries, which grow low to the ground.'[47] Among many workers, no matter how short in stature, strawberries have become known as 'fruit of the devil' (*la fruta del diablo*), since they result in what might literally be crippling labour. Pickers who kneel for hours on the ground are subject to 'Strawberry pickers foot drop', a form of nerve palsy (similarly, blueberry harvesters are susceptible to 'Rakers' wrist' tendinitis).[48] In Greece in 2013, strawberry picking became even more dangerous when 28 strawberry pickers from Bangladesh were shot by farmers after they demanded six months' back pay for their work at a farm in Manolada in the southern Peloponnese. Their harvest became known as 'blood strawberries'.[49]

Cranberry harvest in New Jersey, United States.

Everyman's Right

Freely picking sweet fruits in the wild is a cornerstone of the right to gather, or 'everyman's right',[50] defended staunchly by those great berry-loving nations of northern Europe – the Swedes, Norwegians and Finns. The concept of public access to land is rooted in Scandinavian culture and history, and by the end of the nineteenth century, was enshrined in law. 'Everyman's right' gives everyone 'the basic right to roam freely in the countryside, without needing to obtain permission, no matter who owns or occupies the land.' It also includes the right to forage, even if the berries (or mushrooms or flowers) are on private land.[51] Bilberries, blueberries, wild strawberries, raspberries, lingonberries (also known as the 'red gold of the forests' and a distant relative of the cranberry) and cloudberries, the ethereal fruit of wet peat bogs, are there for anyone's picking (though harvesting of the rare cloudberries can be regulated). 'Everyman's right' is of course more properly every woman's as well. Traditional association of women with plants, particularly roots and berries, and their culinary transformation, meant that historically women and children made up the majority of northern gatherers. Most people still pick for their own use, and consume their lingonberries, bilberries and other soft fruits fresh, in sauces and preserves, or baked into cakes and tarts. Berries continue to be popular design motifs on everything from fabrics to stamps, but wild berry picking has declined in Scandinavia. Even in Finland, where over half of the population continues to reap the wild harvest each year,[52] there is concern that younger people are less interested in berry picking and more inclined to berry buying. In 2015 a record 64.5 million kilograms (142 million lbs) of wild berries were picked, but not all by Finns. A fifth of the bumper crop was collected by 'berry entrepreneurs' who sell the berries in urban markets or export them to consumers as far away as Japan. Since 'everyman's right' applies to individual rights, it also applies to non-residents, and beginning in 2005, thousands of Thais have descended seasonally on Finland (and Sweden) to pick the 'red gold' of the

Dorothea Lange, 'Farm mother of Japanese ancestry picking strawberries
a few days prior to evacuation', November 1942.

forests and the paler gold of the cloudberries. Working thirteen-hour
days for three months and living in abandoned housing, these pickers
have been called slave labour by indignant Swedes and Finns, but for
the Thais, mostly men, berry picking is an opportunity to earn substantial sums. When the harvests are poor, however, many return
home empty-handed, and the Thai government has warned its citi-
zens against seeking their fortunes in the Finnish forests.[53] Ukrainians
and Bulgarians also work the strawberry fields (with European Union
protection) – the northern arm of the migrant berry armies. In the
near future, as immigration laws and borders tighten, everyman and
everywoman in the fields will also include every robot. The Harvest
Croo (Computerized Robotic Optimized Obtainer) may soon replace
the human crew.[54] One of a number of robot pickers being developed
in Europe, Asia and the Americas, the promoters insist they will not
displace human labourers (who pick to a higher standard), but they
will save berries from rotting in the fields from lack of delicate human
fingers to pluck them.[55]

Christopher Switzer, title page to John Parkinson, *Paradisi in sole, paradisus terrestris* (1629), featuring Adam and Eve in Paradise. Eve is plucking a strawberry.

four
Garden Varieties
꙰

Throughout their recorded history, berries have rarely been the objects of deliberate cultivation. Eating berries in season was an evanescent delight, and those who wanted to prolong the pleasure tried to shorten the distance between field or forest and kitchen. The fragrant wood strawberry, the seeming paragon of fruits, was first cultivated in the gardens of French monasteries and in 1368, planted in the hundreds at the Louvre for Charles v by Jean Dudoy, the royal gardener. By the sixteenth century, strawberries were promoted to gardeners in France, Italy and England. Olivier de Serre in *Le Théâtre d'agriculture et mesnage des champs* recommended them as suitable for ornamental gardens both for their flowers and their fruit, and also provided instructions for care and management to increase the size of the diminutive *Fragaria vesca* of the woodlands. Francis Bacon provided similar instructions to English gardeners who wished to plant their 'heath' gardens 'to a natural wildness':

> Trees I would have none in it, but some thickets made only of sweet-briar and honeysuckle, and some wild vine amongst. And the ground set with violets, strawberries, and primroses. For these are sweet and prosper in the shade.

He also advised on creating little 'heaps' with 'bushes pricked upon their top'. Here, the 'standards' were to be 'roses, juniper, holly, berberries (but here and there, because of the smell of their blossoms),

Jacques Le Moyne de Morgue, 'Strawberry', c. 1585, watercolour.

red currants, gooseberries, rosemary, bays, sweetbriar, and such like.'[1] In Bacon's garden, berries were used as ornamentals. The seventeenth-century English kitchen garden, at least as designed by John Parkinson (author of *Paradisi in sole paradisus terrestris; or, A Garden of All Sorts* (1629)), included only one culinary berry – the strawberry. He recommended the leaves and juice for medicinal use, while the berries themselves, he said, are often brought to the Table as a reare service, whereunto claret wine, creame or milke is added with sugar, as every one liketh; as also at other times, both with the better and meaner sort, and are a good cooling and pleasant dish in the hot Summer season.[2]

A Better Berry

The garden strawberry was cultivated so that it was not only closer to the table, but bore larger berries. In *The Gardener's Labyrinth*, Thomas Hill, another early proponent of strawberry culture, opined that the berry 'requires small labour, but, by diligence of the gardener, becometh so great that the same yieldeth faire and big berries as the berries of the bramble in the hedge.'[3] In America, the strawberries were naturally bigger. Growing wild from Hudson's Bay to Louisiana, the Virginia strawberry (*F. virginiana*), in keeping with its 'New World' origin, was a larger, more robust berry than its European counterpart, and twice the size of its dainty relative, the native American woodland strawberry (*F. vesca* ssp. *americana*). Robert Beverley assessed the prolifically growing strawberries of Virginia 'as delicious as any in the World'; they were, in fact, 'so plentiful, that very few Persons take care to transplant them, but can find enough to fill their baskets . . . in the deserted old Fields.'[4] The Virginia strawberry's girth may have increased when brought under the gardener's thumb, but its flavour was said to suffer, so that wild berries continued to be preferred by connoisseurs. While it may not have been a common sight in American gardens, the Robins – gardeners to Louis XIII – included the Virginia in their 1624 catalogue of the *Jardin du roy*, though Parkinson described the American strawberry as large of leaf but not bearing 'kindly' in its new home across the Atlantic without special care.[5]

Size was one of the most desirable attributes of the garden strawberry, and the biggest strawberries of all were discovered by Europeans in South America (also home to the giant *zarzamora* blackberry). The wild strawberries of Chile (*F. chiloensis*) had been grown by Mapuche and Huilliche gardeners long before 1557 when the Spanish-Incan historian Garcilaso de la Vega described a fruit called the *chili*, and which he thought 'of excellent taste and very good to eat'. The *chili* grew 'on low plants, almost crawling on the ground; it has a berry like the arbutus, and is the same size but not round, longer, and shaped like a heart' – a perfect description of the strawberry. According to a missionary who lived in Chile until 1641, most fruits were free for the picking, even in gardens, but 'strawberries, which are called *Frutilla*, are sold. Although I saw them growing wild for miles, they are very expensive when cultivated.' More remarkably, 'In size they are as large as pears and are mostly red, but in the territory of Concepción there are also white and yellow ones.'[6] Amédée-François Frézier, whose name and history became entwined with the Chilean berry, described their cultivation in 1712:

> They are found in the little valley plains where one can conduct a small stream to water them, as is done for the fields in several places in France, because it only rains in Chile during two months of the year, during three at most, in the wintertime . . . The berries are brought back in such abundance to the city of Concepción and the vicinity that people sell them at the market like other fruits. For half a real, which is the lowest money, one gets one or two dozens, wrapped in a cabbage leaf.[7]

A dozen in a 'pottle' is a far cry from the petite European berries, of which that strawberry-loving gardener Thomas Jefferson said one hundred would fill 'half a pint'.[8] Frézier acquired a number of plants, describing the fruit as 'as big as a Walnut, and sometimes as a Hen's Egg, of a whitish Red', but unfortunately 'somewhat less delicious of taste than our Wood Strawberries'. Nevertheless, he contrived to nurse five living specimens through the six-month return voyage to France in 1714. One of these he presented to Antoine de Jussieu, 'to cultivate in the King's Garden'.[9] Philip Miller, the English gardener whose own attempts at cultivating the *chili* in the 1730s met with very indifferent success, was amazed that the Chilean strawberry 'has produced Fruit several Years in the Royal Garden at Paris, where Monsieur Jussieu assured me, it was commonly as large as a small Apple'.[10] Frézier, in his eagerness to bring specimens of the plant with the largest fruit, had collected only female plants. Without the

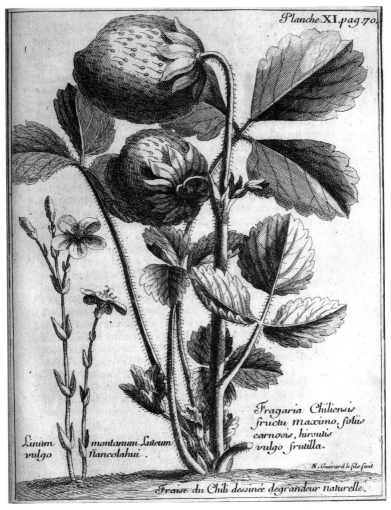

Nicolas Guérard, 'Chilean Strawberry Drawn at Natural Size', in Amédée-François Frézier, *A Voyage to the South-sea* (1735 edn).

male plants to fertilize them, the Chilean plants were barren. That they flourished in Paris and in the area of Plougastel near Brest (where Frézier's own specimens were likely planted) was the result of chance encounters with the male plants of *F. virginiana* or *F. moschata*, common in gardens there. The dioecious nature of strawberries remained a mystery until a young French naturalist, Antoine Nicolas Duchesne, began to study the *Fragaria*. In 1764 the nineteen-year-old, who was the protégé of the royal botanist Bernard de Jussieu, the head of the Jardin du roi in Paris, presented Louis XIV with a splendid example of *F. chiloensis* bearing enormous fruits. Recognizing that the Chilean plant was a female, Duchesne had fertilized it with pollen from the male musky strawberry. Other gardeners had often assumed these male plants were also barren, leading them to tear them out of gardens, thereby ensuring the sterility of the remaining female plants. By 1766 Duchesne had not only described ten species and eight varieties of strawberry in his *Histoire naturelle des fraisiers*, but had unravelled the origin of the 'pine' (*F. x ananassa*) or the 'ananas', a large-fruited strawberry with a pineapple flavour, odour and shape. Duchesne surmised it was 'a cross of the Scarlet strawberry (*F. virginiana*) and the Frutillar (Chilean)', since it shared the characteristics of both. The 'pineapple' was well known in the botanical gardens of Holland, England and France. The inadvertent planting by avid gardeners of two exotics, the Chilean and Virginian, had resulted in the plant that is the ancestor of modern cultivars and is, fortunately for strawberry growers, a hermaphrodite. By 1755, in his supplement to *Histoire*, Duchesne had identified a number of varieties of the pine including the Bath, the Canterbury and the Carolina. The pine went on to become the ancestor of innumerable cultivars, including the redoubtable Hovey and the Keens Seedling.

To size, flavour and productivity as desirable characteristics of the strawberry, the nineteenth-century market gardeners added durability. In 1806 Michael Keens, a grower in Isleworth, London, sowed the seed of a White Chili and discovered one of the seedlings produced a strong plant, which though it may have lacked flavour, had large berries sturdy enough to withstand transport into London. In 1819 Keens raised an even better strawberry from this 'Imperial' seed, the 'Keens Seedling'. With berries up to 5 centimetres (2 in.) in diameter, a deep-red colour and a succulent flavour, this strawberry was a sensation. It also shipped well. European varieties did not, however, fare so well across the Atlantic. Before 1820 most North American nurseries continued to carry imported pines and chilis, but they remained garden curiosities, unable to withstand the rigours of the climate. It was the native Virginian that dominated the strawberry fields of America until 1851, when James Wilson, a Scottish nurseryman living near Albany, New York, came across a particularly splendid specimen of the pine in his strawberry garden. He had sowed seeds of the Hovey, Black Prince and Ross' Phoenix – popular garden varieties at the time – and all pines. What they produced was a self-pollinating plant laden with large fruits and requiring little in the way of special cultivation. More importantly, 'It was very firm, and could be shipped to distant markets under the trying conditions of transportation and marketing that prevailed

Strawberry shipping box label, Wm. Everdell's Sons, NY, c. 1868.

J. Watts after Augusta Withers, 'The Keens Seedling Strawberry', engraving in the *Pomological Magazine* (1829).

then.' The Wilson, as it came to be known, transformed American strawberry growing from the finicky business of the professional gardener to 'a fruit for the millions'.[11] By the 1870s it was estimated that 90 per cent of the strawberries grown in America were Wilsons. It was not, however, without blemish. One critic declared he 'would as soon eat a turnip as a Wilson strawberry', while Henry Ward Beecher, a celebrated preacher, condemned 'this vixenish berry' with religious fervour:

It is the wickedest berry that was ever indulged with liberty. It is an invention by which the producers make money out of the consumer's misery. It has every quality of excellence except in the matter of eating . . . I call upon the Society for the Prevention of Cruelty to Animals to unite with me, and with all rational beings, in suppressing the Wilson's Albany Seedling Strawberry.[12]

Despite its critics, and its somewhat sour taste, the Wilson held sway until the 1880s and was largely responsible for the estimated hundred-fold growth in cultivation during the 'strawberry craze'. As the industry moved south to Florida and west to California, it required a different kind of berry that could withstand southern heat as well as refrigerated transportation. Duchesne, who had championed the delicate perfume and taste of the wild woods strawberry, would have emptied his pottle at the new varieties of large, hard, durable and flavourless berries that the nurseries developed for the mass market.

Gooseberry Fool

The history of the strawberry is somewhat exceptional among berries. While other berries were valued at table, they were often less strenuously nurtured. No other berry graces Parkinson's kitchen garden, but in his orchard, among the apples, peaches, pears and plums, he plants raspberries, gooseberries, berberries and currants, both red and black. Raspberries are eaten 'in the Summer time, as an afternoones dish, to please the taste of the sicke as well as the sound', while currants refresh 'an hot stomacke in the heate of the yeare'. Gooseberries are to be eaten at pleasure, particularly by pregnant women, 'to stay their longings'. The Cornell berries (*Cornus mas*) are preserved and eaten 'both for rarity and delight', but mulberries that stain the fingers and lips are not much desired. The Strawberry tree, 'for all the ancient Writers doe report, that the fruit hereof being eaten, [it] is an enemy to the stomacke and head'.[13] Two hundred years

Catalogue for Woodlawn Nurseries, Rochester, New York, spring 1901.

later, gooseberries, raspberries and currants joined strawberries to dominate the berry markets and the nurseries of Victorian England. Amateurs and professionals alike planted seeds, searched for the most productive plants and the biggest berries, manually pollinated their charges and produced a bewildering number of varieties.

The 1842 *Catalogue of the Fruits Cultivated in the Garden of the Horticultural Society of London* lists hundreds of varieties grown in the Society's gardens, as well as those considered 'inferior' and no longer in cultivation. The catalogue listed 26 varieties (and 76 discarded cultivars) of strawberries, with names descriptive of their parentage and appearance, such as Grimstone Scarlet and Sir Joseph Banks' Scarlet, Hudson's Bay and Pine Roseberry, Downton and Gibb's Black Seedling, Black Prince and Bullock's Blood, Mulberry and Old Pine or Carolina, Surinam or Turner's Pine, Large Blush Chili and Brown Hautbois, Round-fruited Muscatelle and Vineuse de Champagne. (In France, where breeding was stimulated by the introduction of the Keens Seedling in 1824, berries often bore more aristocratic titles – Comte de Paris and Princesse Royale, Vicomtesse Héricart de Thury, Duc de Malakoff, Madame Lebreton and General Chanzy.) There were far fewer varieties of currants – only thirteen – with more prosaic names such as Common Black, Red Dutch and Pearl White. There was only one listed variety of mulberry – the Common – and eight of raspberries, though their names were somewhat more descriptive: Bromley Hill, Cornish, Double-bearing, Old White and Woodward's Red Globe. But the gooseberries! There were 149 varieties of gooseberry and almost the same number deemed unworthy for their garden by the Society. Gooseberry growers were an imaginative and hopeful group, judging by the names they bestowed on their progenies. Some were named after their breeders, such as Barclay's Green and Bates's Favourite, while others were more descriptive of origin or appearance, like Small Hairy Green, Royal White, Smooth Scotch, Lancashire Lad, Red Rose, Pigeon's Egg and Irish Plum. Some had aristocratic pretensions, like their French cousins – Marchioness of Downshire, Lovart's Queen Caroline and Sampson's Queen Ann, Princesse Royale and Boardman's Prince Regent (but also Smith's Radical). Others seemingly embodied the ambitions of the nation; how else to explain Blomerley's John Bull, Bells's Robin Hood, Farrow's Roaring Lion, Royal Oak and Denny's Shakespear, Wellington's Glory and Sydney's Waterloo, Nelson's Waves and Northern Hero, and Massey's Heart of Oak.

If strawberry growing was a craze in America, it was the gooseberry that was the particular passion of the English (and the Scots). The French, of course, grew and ate gooseberries, particularly as a sauce with mackerel,[14] but apparently did not appreciate their finer qualities:

> there exists a strong prejudice against this fine fruit, which prevents the Parisians from giving the improved kinds a fair trial: they have no idea that it is possible that gooseberries should form an excellent article of the dessert; they think of them only as fit for making tarts, or sauce for mackrel![15]

But the British doted on them. Imported from the Continent during the reign of the rose and lily queen Elizabeth I, and then brought within the orchard or garden walls by the seventeenth century, they were found to thrive in the cool moist weather of the Midlands, northern England and Scotland. Most gooseberries were reproduced by cuttings, though they could, of course, be grown from seed. More intensive cultivation called forth new colours, shapes and flavours, and by 1740 the first Gooseberry Clubs were formed. Prizes were offered for the largest and heaviest gooseberries, and fanciers, who referred to their plants as 'pets', developed techniques and stratagems for maximizing their berries' girth and weight, from liquid manure to judicious pruning and attentive coddling of the delicate fruits. Most popular in the industrial areas of Lancashire, Cheshire, Staffordshire, Nottinghamshire, Derbyshire and the West Riding, the clubs catered to the burgeoning interests in natural history and the 'fancy' of mechanics and working men. While others might raise pigeons, horses or rabbits for show, gooseberry fanciers – and in contrast to the pickers, they were almost all men – could use the cottage garden to nurture their leafy pets. The hobby became so popular that by the late eighteenth century, there was a national publication dedicated to gooseberry shows and the celebrated champion berries. Most contests were held in a local public house with prizes of money or sometimes a kettle or set of spoons awarded to the winner. An extract from the *Gooseberry Growers' Register* from 1851 gives the tenor of the events:

> There will be a gooseberry show held at Mr George Wilkinson's, Coach and Horses Inn, Ardsley, near Barnsley; meetings to be agreed upon by the members. There will be a gooseberry show at the house of Mr Robert Howard, Railway Inn, Droylsden, near Ashton-under-Lyne. First meeting, on New-Year's-Day; making-up, Saturday before Easter Sunday. The landlord will give £2., and Mr Joseph Hilton will give £1., towards eight steward's prizes; £1 for the first prize; three 10s. and four kettles. Day of weighing, first Saturday in August; subscription, 4s.; and 9d. each meeting for liquor.[16]

Weighmen assessed the berries with the precision of jewellers, using 'troy' weights (as for gold) and scales accurate enough to weigh a feather. Charles Darwin, investigating variation in domestic species, became something of a fancier himself and grew 54 varieties. He recorded that wild gooseberries were said to weigh about 8 grams (¼ oz); by 1786 fanciers had doubled their weight. By 1830 'Teazer' was more than six times the weight of its wild progenitor, and in 1852 the gargantuan 'London' berry, winner of 333 prizes, weighed in at 896 grains (58 g or 2 oz), the size of a small apple. The precise records in *The Register* allowed Darwin to chart the steady increase in growth that he attributed to improved techniques of cultivation but 'in main part due to the continued selection of seedlings which have been found to be more and more capable of yielding such extraordinary

J. Watts after Augusta Withers, 'Crompton's Sheba Queen Gooseberry',
in the *Pomological Magazine* (1828).

The author and botanist Catharine Parr Traill called the wild gooseberries a cheap luxury for new settlers in the log shanties of Upper Canada. Titus Hibbert Ware, *Two Shanties on the Coldwater Road, Orillia Township*, 1844, watercolour over pencil.

fruit', a neat demonstration of his thinking on the role of selection in art and nature.[17] From its heyday in Darwin's time, when there were 161 shows in 1861, the popularity of the hobby declined; today there remain only a few growers clubs in England, and one in Sweden.[18]

The British took their taste for gooseberries to the Americas, where early settlers in Canada and the United States found native plants growing in the woods. Catherine Parr Traill, who emigrated to the backwoods of Upper Canada in 1832, found the fruit of the wild gooseberry 'spiny' and 'troublesome to gather' but sought out by set-tlers 'as a welcome addition to their scanty fare'. Green, the berries were made into pies and puddings, 'or, when softened, mixed with sugar and milk'. Ripe, they made unsatisfactory preserves, due to 'the harshness of the bristly skin', but as she noted with resignation, 'it was one of the cheap luxuries that found a welcome place at the shanty table'.[19] The native American gooseberry was also resistant to mildew, which plagued introduced European varieties. Hybrids produced by American breeders blended the best of both in sturdy new cultivars. Gooseberries were never, however, as popular as they were in Britain, possibly because even the hybrids produced smaller berries, unsuitable for prize-giving, and also because the plants harboured white pine blister rust. This disease was introduced from Europe, and its host plants were currants and gooseberries. The great American pines were protected – first for shipbuilding and then for lumber – and gooseberries banned, so that generations of children grew up never smelling the cat pee odour of fresh black currants, or tasting the sweet sour of a green gooseberry or, better still, enjoying the summer delight of a gooseberry fool. Hannah Glasse, the paragon of eighteenth-century home cooks, advised her readers on how to make a proper fool:

> To Make a Gooseberry Fool
> Take two quarts of gooseberries, set them on the fire in about a quart of water. When they begin to simmer, and turn yellow, and begin to plump, throw them into a cullender to drain the water out; then with the back of a spoon carefully squeeze the pulp, throw the sieve into a dish, make them pretty sweet, and let them stand till they are cold. In the mean time take two quarts of new milk, and the yolks of four eggs, beat up with a little grated nutmeg; stir it softly over a slow fire, when it begins to simmer, take it off, and by degrees stir it into the gooseberries. Let it stand till it is cold, and serve it up. If you make it with cream, you need not put any eggs in: and if it is not thick enough, it is only boiling more gooseberries. But that you must do as you think proper.[20]

Taming the Wild Blueberry

If most North Americans never ate a gooseberry fool, they had their share of blueberry pies and huckleberry puddings. As Thoreau had rhapsodized, 'What should we think of a summer in which we did not taste a huckleberry pudding? That is to Jonathan what his plum pudding is to John Bull.'[21] Blueberries, and the huckleberries with which they were often confused, were first appreciated as a kind of substitute for currants or raisins, both fresh or dried and mixed

Frederick Vernon
Coville, Chief
Botanist of the
USDA (1867–1937).

into puddings, a practice perhaps adopted from the Indigenous inhabitants. The first recipe for blueberry pie, now almost as American as apple pie, appeared in 1850.[22] Thankfully, the wild blueberries that filled the pie shells were abundant, since they were notably resistant to cultivation and improvement. Growers would uproot the hardy plants, lavish attention and manure on them and watch them wilt and die. It was only in 1911, late in the timeline of berry cultivation, that the United States Department of Agriculture (USDA) published *Experiments in Blueberry Culture*. After years of failures, Frederick Vernon Coville, Chief Botanist at the USDA, realized that blueberries did not appreciate the rich alkaline soils that farmers tried so hard to ensure for most crops. Nor did they appreciate manuring; what a

The brown waters of the Pine Barrens, Whitesbog, New Jersey.

blueberry wanted, contrary to 'all the fundamental principles of agriculture', was a soil 'so acid that ordinary plants die of poison and starvation', an environment, he noted, similar to that of cranberry bogs. Coville's findings found a receptive reader in Elizabeth White, daughter of one of the nation's largest cranberry growers, who had grown up in cranberry country. Reading Coville's book gave her 'an entirely new view of [her] old friends, the huckleberry bushes and cranberry vines':

> To me it was the most fascinating reading for never before had I known that the soil of our bogs was acid, as was the water of our streams, that it was this which made our bog water brown . . . Never before had I known that associated with the roots of blueberry, cranberry and most other plants which grow in acid soils is a symbiotic fungus which in some still unexplained way assists these plants in obtaining the nitrogen necessary for their growth.[23]

White invited Coville to work with her to grow a better blueberry. Coville noted in his report that 'From the market standpoint the features of superiority in a blueberry' were size, colour, 'dryness' and plumpness. He also remarked that if blueberries were to be cultivated, the high cost of picking by hand meant securing a good-sized berry: 'Large size and abundance mean a great reduction in the cost of picking.'[24] Blueberries were also not self-fertile and required cross-pollination. In 1911 Coville crossed a highbush with a lowbush plant to create two hybrids that he named Brooks and Russell.[25] Over the next two years, he bred more than 3,000 hybrids, many based on plants obtained from the wild by White. Relying on the local knowledge of her neighbours, the New Jersey 'Pineys' as they were called, White collected exemplary bushes of the swamp or highbush blueberry (*Vaccinium corymbosum*) for the breeding programme. Coville and White proceeded by trial and error, working on what they called their 'experimental farm in miniature' at Whitesbog. Size was important, but they found that some large berries were mealy in texture; others would crack open when it rained or had skins that were too tough. They tore out and burned thousands of bushes. By 1916 they had planted a field of 1,000 hybrid seedlings, and in 1918 they sold their first berries. In 1921 they had 6.5 hectares (16 ac) of blueberry test fields, with 27,000 different hybrid seedlings. Of these, 18,000 hybrid plants bore fruit, and from this grand assemblage, they selected four hybrids for sale to other growers. The wild blueberry had been tamed. In 1915 Whitesbog blueberries earned $37 per acre; by 1920 they earned $1,280 per acre, and the berries were 19 mm (¾ in.) in diameter, the size of a Concord grape. The hand-picked berries were packaged in clear cellophane imported from Europe and sold at a premium in the New York market. Elizabeth White became known as the 'Blueberry Queen' and the Whitesbog berries as 'Jewels of the Moorland'. Although she and Coville went their separate ways, she continued to work to develop plants with fruit of consistent size that could be more easily harvested and mechanically sorted. In 1923 it was reported that 'unscrupulous dealers are said to be selling inferior wild blueberries for grafted hybrids of high quality'.[26] The cultivated berry had triumphed over its tiny-fruited ground-hugging cousin *Vaccinium pennsylvanicum*, what Thoreau had called 'that most Olympian fruit of all — delicate flavored, thin-skinned and cool'.[27] Today it is the untamed, intensely flavoured wild berry that demands a premium price, and size doesn't matter.

Cranberry Culture

American cranberries were the staple of the Blueberry Queen's family business. The large marsh cranberry *Vaccinium macrocarpon* grew in acidic bogs and swamps from Newfoundland to New England and from Wisconsin to Arkansas, as well as in the cool Pacific Northwest. Until the early nineteenth century, supplying American households with the makings of cranberry sauce or the filling for cranberry pies had largely depended on wild berries picked by hand. In 1810 Henry Hall, a farmer in Cape Cod, Massachusetts, observed that natural berries grew more plentifully in areas covered by wind-blown sand. Hall decided to transplant vines and sod into a bog he drained and then sanded. The berries thrived, and the American cranberry industry was born. Growers ditched, drained, sanded and flooded to encourage the berries' growth. In the 1860s cranberry fever blossomed, encouraging speculators to get into the business, digging up swamps and marshlands for a new kind of red gold. As a New Jersey paper reported with capitalistic glee,

> The people of Ocean County are going into the cranberry business this spring with a vigor and enthusiasm that completely overshadows all former efforts in that line. Vast swamps are being cleared and the prospect is that thousands of acres will be planted. There is no doubt that there is money in it.[28]

There was indeed money to be made in berries; the Whites of Whitesbog became a veritable dynasty of successful cranberry culturists. Joseph White, father of the redoubtable Elizabeth, published *Cranberry Culture* in 1870, passing along his family's hard-learned methods for avoiding berry rot, using flooding to exterminate pests, picking and packing, and rolling the berries to separate sound from

'During the picking process many of the cranberries are torn from the vines and fall to the ground. The bogs are then flooded and agitated with the hydroplane which causes the cranberries to float, Burlington County, New Jersey.' photograph by Arthur Rothstein, October 1938.

bad (rotten berries didn't roll well). The cranberries brought within these new wet gardens were primarily wild plants, selected for colour, size and productivity by farmers themselves. The Early Black variety was first raised in Massachusetts in 1835 and is still grown for market. McFarlin was a named variety selected from a bog in South Carver, Massachusetts, in 1874, and Potter from a bog in Wisconsin in 1890. When, in the 1920s, the great cranberry fields were afflicted with 'false blossom', a parasitical disease carried by a leafhopper, the United States Department of Agriculture began an organized breeding programme, seeking varieties resistant to the insect. Subsequently, breeding criteria turned towards bigger, brighter, firmer

Eastman Johnson, *The Cranberry Harvest, Island of Nantucket*, 1880, oil on canvas.

berries, and in the 1950s the USDA introduced Stevens, an offspring of the wild McFarlin and Potter varieties and now the most widely used cranberry in cultivation.[29]

Berries had to be firm to withstand the new machinery of cultivation and harvesting. Until the 1920s, berries were picked from dry fields by the nimble fingers of women and children or scooped by strong men using heavy wooden boxes armed with steel teeth. They were replaced by 'Improved Cranberry Picking Machines', tractor-like devices armed with revolving combs, and by the 1950s, despite losses of 20 to 30 per cent of unharvested berries, fifteen men guiding smaller lawnmower-sized machines through the fields could replace 150 pickers. Even fewer workers were needed once the technique of wet harvesting took over the fields. Cranberries contain tiny pockets of air, and when the vast commercial bogs are flooded, the berries pop to the surface, where they are 'beaten' from the vine and corralled for harvest. Wet cranberries are, however, more susceptible to rot than those picked dry, so that cranberries are now more likely to come processed in a can than packed into a wooden box.

Boysenberry, Poisonberry

The blackberry has been called 'a primitive thug that has been turning parts of the northern hemisphere into off-limit areas since well before the last Ice Age began, some thirty-five thousand years ago.'[30] While a little unjust, the wild blackberry (*Rubus* sp.) is widespread and prolific. *Rubus* species are found on all continents except Antarctica; the greatest number of species is found in Eurasia and North America, where they abound in woods and thickets, creating the famous bramble bushes that tear your clothes and stain your hands. Their cousins the raspberries are equally well distributed, though the latter have been, historically, more prized for their flavour and have been cultivated in European gardens since the 1500s. Because they are so widespread and abundant (and invasive), little effort was made to bring blackberries and their ilk into more orderly cultivation until Luther Burbank took them under his exceptionally green thumb. Burbank was an American plant breeder and horticulturalist of great ability and superabundant energy. In his half-century career (which only ended with his death in 1926), he developed more than eight hundred strains and varieties of plants, from the Shasta Daisy to the Santa Rosa plum and the Russet Burbank potato. He had a particular fondness for berries, which he saw as the 'Cinderella of the pomological family'. A disciple of Darwinian selection, he solicited varieties from around the world and bred, crossbred and backcrossed thousands of seedlings on 8-hectare (20 ac) plots, ruthlessly ripping out and discarding those

Luther Burbank
(1849–1926)
examining poppies.

that did not meet his vision of what a fruit might be. His breedings
were anything but controlled – he kept few notes of his crosses – and
some were most unusual, such as apples with blackberries or strawberries with raspberries. One of his most contentious crosses was what
he purported to be the offspring of the great African stubble berry,
Solanum guineense, and the little downy nightshade *S. villosum*. They were
not prepossessing parents, the African berry being vile-tasting and the
nightshade insipid, and they both shared the reputation of solanums
for being suspicious, if not downright poisonous. Burbank called his
new variety 'Sunberry' and sold it to the nurseryman Lewis Childs,
who immediately changed its name to wonderberry and promoted it
with all the enthusiasm of a circus hawker:

E.W. Reid's *Nursery Catalogue*, spring 1896, featuring Burbank's Plum and his Eureka Raspberry.

'Wonderberry' (*Solanum nigrum*).

Luther Burbank's greatest and newest production. Fruit blue-black like an enormous rich blueberry. Unsurpassed for eating . . . in any form. The greatest garden fruit ever introduced . . . Easiest plant in the world to grow, succeeding anywhere and yielding great masses of rich fruit.[31]

Wonderberry was confused by many with deadly nightshade (*Atropa belladonna*), which it resembled, or worse, was reviled as simply a marketing trick to promote not a new hybrid but the black or garden nightshade (*S. nigrum*), which was eaten in Europe, Africa and Asia as well as in the southern U.S. states. Burbank defended his creation by pointing out that the solanums provide the potato, the tomato

Luther Burbank also bred a 'White blackberry. A careful Burbank product of the Lawton and the Crystal-White. Unusually luscious and prolific.' From *Luther Burbank's Bounties from Nature to Man* (1911).

and the aubergine (once equally despised as the *mala insana*) and by emphasizing his variety's culinary qualities. He quoted from an enthusiastic gardener and college professor who wrote to him that, 'One man, an attorney, planted some Sunberries and pulled them up because they looked like nightshade. I completely converted him by sending him a pie.'[32]

Burbank was particularly fond of children, and he also devoted much effort to developing a thornless blackberry, so that little children could gather the dark fruits with impunity. In the 1880s Burbank had imported blackberry seeds from India, unaware that a European blackberry (*R. armeniacus*) had been earlier introduced to India. He subjected the seedlings to his usual regime of crossing and re-crossing, and selected the plants that had the largest fruits and no thorns. He named his 'new improved' variety the 'Himalaya Giant', but unfortunately, like many blackberries, it grew abundantly and exhibited the remarkable genetic variability of its kind, shaking off its cultivated attributes. Soon berry-loving birds were spreading the seeds of these vigorous and thorny blackberries throughout the Pacific Northwest, where they have become a noxious and very prickly pest. He had somewhat better luck with his 'Phenomenal' loganberry. The loganberry was the result of a cross between a raspberry and a blackberry, bred in the garden of a Judge Logan in Santa Cruz, California, in 1881 and released in 1890. Burbank made his own cross in 1894 and released his loganberry in 1905 as the hyperbolically named 'Phenomenal'. It remains in cultivation today, and was one of the parents of yet another new berry, the Youngberry, bred in 1926 by the amateur gardener B. M. Young, who could grow neither 'Loganberry' nor 'Phenomenal' in Louisiana, but triumphed when he crossed 'Phenomenal' with a locally adapted cultivar, 'Austin Mayes'.

These new berries paled in popularity, however, in comparison to the 'boysenberry', discovered on the Lubben farm in Napa County, California, by farmer Rudolph Boysen. When Boysen moved to southern California, he took seedlings with him, but eventually abandoned them and the farm. Somehow, George Darrow of the USDA in Maryland heard of these hybrids with their large, sweet, reddish-purple berries and like Coville and White, Darrow and local nurseryman Walter Knott set out to find and grow the new blackberry variety. They succeeded, and the rest is horticultural history. By 1932 Knott was selling the berries that he and Darrow named in honour of Rudolph Boysen at a roadside stand, and by 1934, with only one hundred vines, Knott was able to produce 2,200 baskets, each weighing 454 grams (1 lb), of the oversize berry. In the best tradition of the plant showmen, he marketed it with as much hoopla as he could manage, and the *Los Angeles Times* called the boysenberry the 'California-developed king of the bush'. Twenty years later, in 1954, it was the preeminent berry under cultivation in the state, with 970 hectares

Walter and Cordelia Knott outside a replica of their 'Original Berry Stand', *c.* 1969.
Several versions of the stand were built over the decades.

(2,400 ac) growing the purple fruit. Boysenberries were the new fruit of my childhood, and on a trip to California, my mother promised me a taste of the berry sensation at the famous Knott's Berry Farm. What had been a roadside stand had mushroomed into a major attraction on a par with Disneyland. Its transformation began when Walter Knott built the Chicken Dinner Restaurant in 1934, where Mrs Knott served fried chicken and her signature Boysenberry Pies. So popular was her cooking that local residents came in droves; Walter decided to offer them some amusements to while away the long wait for dinner. By the end of the 1950s, the family farm had become Knott's Berry Farm and Ghost Town, with a Haunted Shack, the Calico Saloon, a Stage Coach Ride and Boot Hill Cemetery, a vision of the Wild West as American as boysenberry pie.

five
Preserving the Harvest
❦

Let nature do your bottling, as also your
pickling and preserving.

HENRY DAVID THOREAU, 'HUCKLEBERRIES'

Henry David Thoreau was a great believer in living locally
and eating seasonally. He advised that one should 'Grow
green with spring, yellow and ripe with autumn. Drink of
each season's influence as a vial, a true panacea of all remedies mixed
for your especial use.' While he extolled the 'vials of summer' found in
the wild grape, he abjured those stored in the cellar. 'Drink the wines',
he said, 'not of your own, but of Nature's bottling – not kept in goat-
or pig-skin, but in the skin of a myriad fair berries.'[1] Unfortunately, in
the temperate regions where the soft fruits of summer flourish, these
sylvan quaffs are only available for a short season, and berry lovers
have for millennia sought to preserve summer's savours into the long,
dark winter. Some fruits keep better than others. The Romans tucked
apples into honey, and stored grapes in barrels of distilled water or
buried in barley so that they could eat them out of season.[2] In the
collection of recipes attributed to the Roman epicure Apicius, there
is a method for preserving mulberries by 'laying' them in their own
juice mixed with new wine in a glass vessel, and boiling the mixture to
reduce to half, making, one assumes, a kind of syrupy preserve without
sugar or honey. Similarly, berries often provided the only sweeteners
in a traditional diet for Indigenous people. In North America, whole

berries would be dried in the sun or over smouldering fires (low heat helped to preserve their vitamin content), or pounded into cakes and pemmican. Some firmer berries, such as elderberries, cranberries or soapberries, were stored in containers under water or a layer of oil, sweetening over the winter.[3] The seventeenth-century Recollect missionary and chronicler Gabriel Sagard noted that in New France, the Hurons would dry their blueberries for winter, 'as we do prunes in the sunn'. In New England, Roger Williams, in his account published in 1643, says that 'currants [grapes and whortleberries] dried by the natives' are 'preserved all the year' and then 'they beat to powder and mingle it with their parched meal, and make a delicate dish which they call Sautauthig, which is as sweet to them as plum or spice cake to the English.'[4] Like the Inuit, Laplanders would bury delicate cloudberries (*Rubus chamaemorus*) under the snow to preserve them, or boil them with fish into soft jellies. In Australia, a country where cold storage is not a natural option, the small berries of the bush tomato (*Solanum centrale*) are allowed to dry on the bush before harvesting. In South America, particularly in the berry-rich highlands of Ecuador, Chile and Peru, the Andean blueberry or *mortiño* (*Vaccinium floribundum*) could often be gathered twice a year and was often eaten fresh or in porridges and juices, the double harvest making long-term preservation less necessary.

Berries, despite their ubiquity and sweetness, seemed of minor interest to medieval European cooks. Most recipes calling for fruits refer to figs, raisins and *raisins de Corinthe*, commonly called currants in English. Grapes, the berries of the vine, have been dried for millennia and were an article of trade throughout the Mediterranean. Berberries too were often dried in India, and widely used there, but the common berries of fields and wood do not appear to have been dried or preserved for culinary use. Fruit is not mentioned at all in the medieval *Libro de arte coquinaria* (The Art of Cooking, *c.* 1465), though vegetables are plentiful. With a few exceptions, only grapes, currants and occasionally gooseberries appear in early recipe books. Among the *Espices qu'il fault* (necessary spices) in the fourteenth-century *Le Viandier* of

Wall painting from the House of Julia Felix in Pompeii, *c.* 70 CE.

Taillevent, *groseilles* (gooseberries) are mentioned as giving a 'green colour'. Currants also serve as a substitute for grapes in a sauce for meat, and for raisins in a stuffing with pine nuts for a chicken.[5]

The English set more store by berries, and in *The Forme of Cury*, written at the end of the fourteenth century (there are multiple manuscripts), there is a recipe for 'murrey' or 'morree', a kind of mulberry pudding.[6] Strawberries were widely available in woods or gardens and enjoyed fresh with milk or cream, but John Gerard in his *Herball* (1636) warned that the 'nourishment they yeeld is little, thin, and waterish', and worse, if they putrefy in the stomach, their 'nourishment is naught'.[7] Small reason to eat them fresh, and fourteenth-century cooks transformed them into something much more palatable by washing them in red wine, and then boiling them in almond milk thickened with starch or rice flour and a flavouring of sugar, saffron, pepper, ginger and cinnamon, which turned the waterish strawberries into a complex spicy custard, studded with Corinth raisins and 'pointed' with vinegar and a little white 'grese'. The concoction was coloured with Alkenade (a red dye, as if the strawberries were not red enough – a practice to be repeated in the twentieth century), and then turned into a bowl and sprinkled with pomegranate seeds, certainly an early form of the puddings that so delighted the English.[8] The country folk of Cheshire apparently also enjoyed black whortleberries in cream or milk, but apothecaries boiled the juice of the vaccinium with honey or sugar until thick, and this was generally much preferred to the raw fruit, which, when eaten, was 'offensive to a weake and cold stomacke', whereas the sweet syrup was not. Similarly, 'fen berries' (*V. oxycoccos*) were much better served as a syrup: 'The juyce of these also is boyled till it be thicke, with suger added that it may be kept, which is good for all things that the berries are, yea, and far better.'[9] In his *Opera dell'arte del cucinare* (1570), Bartolomeo Scappi, chef to popes and princes, provided few recipes for berries – and those were chiefly destined for the sick room – such as red currant sops and sauces of gooseberries, strawberries and mulberries. He acknowledged, however, that red currants might set into a jelly, and suggested strawberries be added in April or May to a goat's-milk pudding. He also substituted gooseberries for verjuice grapes in flavouring tarts of tongue or ortolans, or stuffed them into a crookneck squash with cheese, parsley, cinnamon and sugar.[10]

Jams and Jellies

It was sugar that transformed the berry harvest from a brief seasonal pleasure to a year-round indulgence. Sugar was initially regarded as a spice and was generally available in small quantities in the medieval kitchen, though by the sixteenth century, there are records of aristocratic banquets where not only did it rain sugar candy on guests, but they ate from plates of sugar that could be cracked and consumed. When sugar became widely available and less expensive in the seventeenth century, it replaced honey as the preservative of choice for soft fruits, used in a quantity not dissimilar to that of the contemporary kitchen. It was in France that the office of the *confiseur*, who prepared the innumerable conserves, jellies, compotes, syrups and liquors that filled stillrooms and storerooms, was first celebrated in a book. François Massialot, *chef de cuisine* to innumerable aristocrats,

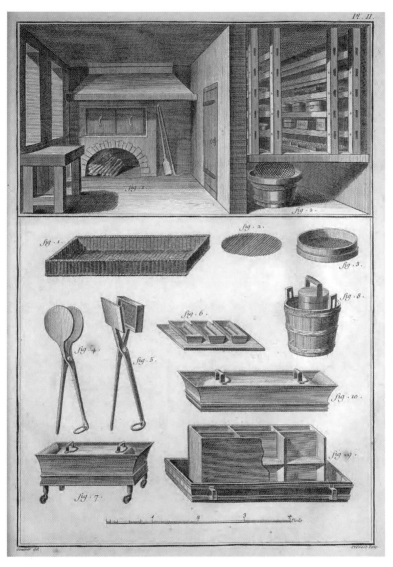

Instruments for the office of *confiseur*, in Denis Diderot and
Jean Le Rond d'Alembert, eds, *Encyclopédie* (1763).

Pâtes de fruits d'Auvergne, traditional fruit pastes made in the district of Saulcet, France.

published *Nouvelle instruction pour les confitures, les liqueurs, et les fruits* in 1692, documenting the vast array of ways the *confiseur* conceived to preserve the harvest.

Berries were only some of the myriad fruits available to the French, who treasured grapes, apples, pears of all sorts, plums, quinces and cherries. The small fruits had, however, an important place in the kitchen and at table, and Massialot enumerated them by month, delighting in green gooseberries in May, followed by sweet wood strawberries, to be enjoyed *dans leur naturel* (just as they are) or in compotes. In June came raspberries, red gooseberries, barberries and, by July, mulberries. What was better, he wrote, than strawberries washed in water or wine, powdered with sugar and turned into basins or porcelain dishes, giving off *une odeur agréable qui charme tout le monde* (an enchanting perfume that charms all). Strawberries, raspberries and gooseberries, of course, could also be served *glacée*, like cherries, and gooseberries could be made into *bouquets de fille* (dainty bouquets) sparkling with sugar. In addition, Massialot devised clever transformations that would preserve the colour, sometimes the shape and certainly the taste of fresh berries. He provided instructions for making compotes that could either be served right away or saved until later. There were *gelées*, conserves, *marmelades* and pastes, the latter thick enough to set when poured into tin moulds in the shape of hearts, squares and fleur-de-lis. (One of my great joys in Paris was to discover a shop that had been making and selling *pâte de fruits* since 1761.) There were transparent *clarequets* and gooseberries made in *façon de Tours*, with an addition of a second boiling of the *marc* left in the sieve after the berries had been strained and pressed. This, Massialot contended, was only worthwhile if there were a sufficient quantity; otherwise, the leftover *marc* went to the children: *car quand il y en a peu, ce font les profits des enfans* (for when there is only a little, the children profit). Making all these preserves meant a lot of sugar, measuring pound for pound, and in the case of pastes, two pounds for every one of fruit. Once prepared, the fragrant, delectable preparations were stored in jars covered with paper and kept cool and dark, ready to be served at a winter meal to bring back a memory of summer.[11]

Mulberries and gooseberries could also be turned into syrups, and the triumvirate of gooseberries, raspberries and strawberries also

A fruit shop lounge, 1786. Note the container marked 'ratafia'.

made refreshing fruit waters, to be drunk in season, or in the case of the latter two, distilled into potent liqueurs. A half to two teaspoons of these delectable elixirs would benefit the heart and the head and purify the blood. The French *confiseur* also made ratafias, heady liquors steeped from cherries and their broken pits (for the bitter almond taste) and spiced with coriander, cinnamon, cloves and long pepper, and then flavoured with strawberry or raspberry syrup or sometimes with gooseberries added to the mix. Black currants, though not much esteemed by cooks, were introduced into gardens from Eastern Europe in the seventeenth century. Despite what Gerard called their 'stinking and somewhat loathing savour',[12] they became one of the components of *ratafia de cassis*, which evolved in the nineteenth century into the celebrated aperitif of Burgundy, crème de cassis.

Preserved berries decorated the best tables. The colourful *marmelades* could also be used in the manner of flowers in a parterre to create patterned desserts. In *Countrey Contentments; or, The English Huswife*, Gervase Markham explained how to create decorative designs on cream tarts, such as beasts or coats of arms using yellow, blue and

Tray with three jam pots, Sèvres porcelain, 1761.

Jam jar of salt-glazed
stoneware, Belper,
1799.

red preserves, conserves, marmalades and 'Goodinyaks' (*cotignacs*).[13]
Massialot also called for compotes in porcelain dishes, and it is possible to imagine ruby-red strawberry compote filling one of the newly
available soft paste porcelain bowls from Saint-Cloud. Berries could
be transformed into sparkling jewels by dipping fresh or gently sim-
mered berries in egg white and then more sugar, creating bunches
of soft fruits that cracked with sweetness. That 'compleat huswife'
of the eighteenth century, Hannah Glasse, preserved 'Cherries with
the Leaves and Stalks green' and said, 'They look very pretty at candle-
light in a desert.'[14]

Home Preserves

Until the middle of the nineteenth century, preserving the small fruits of summer was a domestic enterprise, and a well-stocked cellar a tribute to the housewife's skill. Hannah Glasse wrote not for the professional confectioner but for women who managed their own households and their cooks and servants.[15] She provided her readers with clear instructions and handy tips, including advice on making jellies, conserves, marmalades and 'giam'. Success was measured not only in flavour and appearance but on how well a preserve endured until summer came once more. Glasse put down her berries, quinces, plums and peaches in stone jars or glass bottles, corking them or sealing them, sometimes 'papering them up' with sheets of wet or dry paper, covering them with a layer of oil or filling the jars with brandy, and placing them in a dry place. She insisted that her readers 'always use stone jars' for hot pickles, for despite the initial expense, they keep the pickle better, 'for vinegar and salt will penetrate through all earthen vessels, stone and glass is the only thing to keep pickles in'. She pickled red currants and barberries in a mix of vinegar and sugar, covering the jars with a bladder and leather.[16] She would bottle gooseberries to keep until Christmas, to be served up with the goose:

> To keep Green Gooseberries till Christmas
> Pick your large green gooseberries on a dry day, have ready your bottles clean and dry, fill the bottles and cork them, set them in a kettle of water up to the necks, let the water boil very softly till you find the gooseberries are coddled, take them out, and put in the rest of the bottles till all are done; then have ready some rosin melted in a pipkin, dip the necks of the bottles in, and that will keep all air from coming at the cork, keep them in a cold dry place, where no damp is, and they will bake as red as a cherry. You may keep them without scalding, but then the skins will not be so tender, nor bake so fine.[17]

She also made barrels of powerful raisin wine with brandy and elder-berry syrup, and she appeared to be a dab hand at making the berry wines for which the English housewife was justly famous. She made distillates of raspberries, blackberries, elderberries and red currants, adding white wine or brandy as the recipe demanded, to fortify and preserve the tipple:

> Gather your currants on a fine dry day, when the fruit is full ripe, strip them, put them in a large pan, and bruise them with a wooden pestle till they are all bruised. Let them stand in a pan or tub twenty-four hours to foment; then run it through a hair-sieve, and don't let your hand touch your liquor. To every gallon of this liquor, put two pounds and a half of white sugar, stir it well together, and put it into your vessel. To every six gallons, put a quart of brandy, and let it stand six weeks. If it is fine, bottle it . . .[18]

Strawberry *varenye*, Azerbaijan.

Russia was also famous for its fruit preserves or *varenye*, the cherished products of a short summer. *Varenye* were an essential element in Russian cuisine, eaten with bread or served as a sweetener for tea. Though often translated as 'jam' or 'jelly', these are whole fruit preserves; berries are steeped in hot sugar syrup until soft, similar to Hannah Glasse's gooseberry coddling technique, resulting in jewel-like fruits suspended in a clear liquid tinted red, amber or dark purple by the colour of the fruits. The Russian writer Leo Tolstoy understood that these sweet products of women's labour could be a powerful symbol of domestic order. In *Anna Karenina* (1877), he describes a scene where making berry preserves is about far more than just berries. The women of the Shcherbatsky clan argue with the ageing housekeeper, Agafya Mikhailovna, nurse to Levin, about how to make *varenye*. Levin, whose marriage has brought this new family

Sergei Mikhailovich Prokudin-Gorskii, *Peasant Girls*, Russian Empire, 1909. Three young women offer berries to visitors at their *izba*, a traditional wooden house along the Sheksna River, near the town of Kirillov.

Apollinary Vasnetsov, *Making Jam* (*Za varkoi varen'ya*), 1892, oil on canvas.

into his household, senses the unease between the women, and for an instant sees in the dispute over jam, the 'alien regime of his wife's family'. Agafya Mikhailovna adds water to the berries, as she has always done, but she is overruled by her master's new relations, who insist that the fruits will last better without it. (While Russians could rely on supplies of ice from icehouses as a preservative, even their plentiful resources were melted by the end of berry-picking season.) The imperious princess has the last word: '"Follow my advice, please, and put over each pot of jelly a round piece of paper soaked in rum, and you will not need ice in order to preserve them," said the princess.'[19]

This would certainly also have been the advice of Mrs Haskell, author of a much-praised domestic manual of the American Civil War era, *The Housekeeper's Encyclopedia*. She advised her home cooks to cover their preserves in jars first with tissue paper dipped in brandy, and then sealed with paper wet with beaten egg white and well pressed down. (She wisely counselled a practice that I continue to neglect – mark the contents and date on the cover.)[20] She also dried strawberries, whortleberries, blackberries, raspberries and currants, sealing them into paper bags, but kept her cranberries fresh in a tub of water. She gave instructions for hermetically sealed preserves, which she claimed were 'the first reliable rules published'.[21] She placed whole gooseberries, strawberries, raspberries and currants in tightly corked jars, which were then submerged in cold water and brought up to boiling. She even tinned her own fruits, in a complex process that began by placing fruit and sugar in a can, soldering the lids in place, and then punching a small hole in the lid with an awl and submerging the cans in a hot water bath, finally re-soldering the hole. It seems no surprise, however, that it was a French *confiseur*, Nicolas Appert, who had developed the process of conserving foods in bottles and tins by sealing them tightly and immersing them in boiling water. His process was improved in England and was used from the early 1800s to process foods both for domestic and commercial consumption. In America, packing Maine blueberries in tin cans was the innovation that created the commercial blueberry industry. When

Bernhard Dondorf, *Küche*, no. 80, 1840–70, hand-coloured lithograph, Frankfurt. Note the papered jars in the cupboard.

Will Grefé, 'The Winter Supplies', *Women's World*, Chicago (September 1915).

The Winter *Supplies*

The best ways of putting them up are described in this number

More than Two Million subscribers receive Woman's World every month

WOMAN'S WORLD

September 1915   *Five Cents*

CHICAGO

the local sardine canneries lost their southern markets during the Civil War, they turned to blueberries, shipping the tinned fruit to soldiers of the Union Army to ward off scurvy. But it was the invention of the Mason jar by an American tinsmith in 1858 that made home canning and preserving a simpler and safer business. Threaded zinc caps and later caps with a glass insert could be screwed on to jars, permitting a tight seal. The glass jar and screw cap gradually replaced the older stoneware and ceramic jam pots when jams and jellies became products of mass production.

Factory Fruit

If it was the French who defined the art of *confiserie*, it was the British who industrialized jam-making. The manuals of the eighteenth and nineteenth centuries were directed at those households that could afford both the produce of a home garden and the equipment and labour to make conserves. As more and more people moved from the country to the cities, access to garden produce for the majority of the working classes was restricted to an occasional pottle of gooseberries or substandard strawberries from the costermongers. Even if it were readily and cheaply available, fresh fruit was still regarded by many with some suspicion (see Gerard's comment on eating fresh strawberries), and the working-class diet was monotonous and bland. What could enliven a slab of coarse bread was a little jam.[22] Crosse & Blackwell began as a purveyor of pickles and tinned fish, but in 1841 became the first company to mass-produce jam; by the 1860s they were using 450 tonnes of fruit for jam-making.[23] They were followed into the business by firms such as Pink's (1861), Hartley's (1871), Chivers (1873) and the great marmalade makers (Robertson, Keillor, Cooper's, John Moir & Son). Sugar was heavily taxed in Britain until the 1870s, and the first factories scrimped to make a profit, with reports of jams being produced from the sweepings of the warehouse floors. Physician, chemist and public health advocate Dr Arthur Hill Hassall made a crusade of exposing the nefarious practices of

John Moir & Son, 'Our long experience and unequalled facilities enable us to produce these goods of superior quality', 1870–1900, advertising card, London.

Edward Penfield, drawing for Lewis B. Allyn, 'Pure Food Campaigns,
the Way to Conduct Them', *Collier's Magazine* (5 July 1913).

Victorian preserve manufacturers, who added turnip, pumpkin or
apple to stretch marmalades, copper to make the greengages especially green, and beet juice and logwood to make the strawberries red.
Despite the abundance of the fruit, they made 'raspberry' preserve
from red currants flavoured with orris root. Copper was particularly
present in bottled fruits, as one of Dr Hassall's correspondents attests:

> I had bought a bottle of preserved gooseberries from one of
> the most respectable grocers in this town, and had had its
> contents transferred into a pie. It struck me that the goose-
> berries looked fearfully green when cooked; and on eating
> one with a steel fork, its intense bitterness sent me in search
> of the sugar. After having sweetened and mashed the goose-
> berries with the same steel fork, I was about to convey some
> to my mouth, when I observed the prongs to be completely
> coated with a thin film of bright metallic copper. My testi-
> mony can be borne out by the evidence of three others, two
> of whom dined at my table.[24]

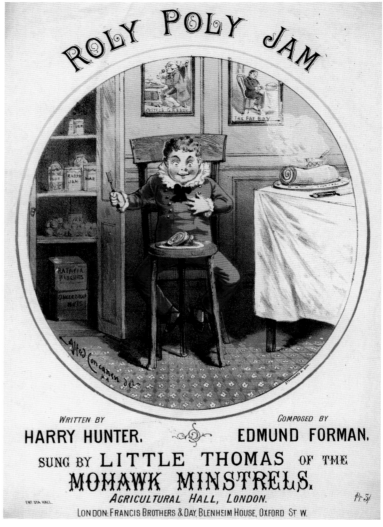

Alfred Concanen, *Roly Poly Jam*, 1859–86, music cover sheet.

Housewives were in fact encouraged to make their own preserves to avoid the hazards and adulterations of commercial products. Thanks to Hassall's exposés, some of the manufacturers improved their practices, but a generation later, it would appear the situation had not improved greatly. In 1873 a Dr Tidy called attention to 3,630 kilograms (8,000 lb) of bad figs seized at the docks. The figs were unsalable, being 'rotten and maggoty', but no matter, they were to be

used in the manufacture of jam together with glue, bad plums, and the sweepings of fruit-warehouses. The seeds and a small quantity of raspberry jam, with which the concoction was mixed, gave the so-called 'preserve' a genuine appearance, and it was largely sold among the poor under the name of 'Family preserve', 'Royal jam', 'Fruit preserve', and 'Household jam'.[25]

Robert Moore Brinkerhoff, 'Let Your Fruit Trees Save Sugar', 1917–19, poster.

When the British Prime Minister Sir William Gladstone promoted fruit farming to replace corn in the 1880s, more manufacturers entered the business. A report in the *British Medical Journal* applauded Gladstone's initiative, as a matter of public health:

> people have begun to discover that the stuff sold as butter is neither palatable nor cheap, and that whereas butter (so-called) costs from 15d. to 20d. a pound, good sound jam can be had for from 7d. to 9d., and we have even tasted very fair raspberry jam, retailed in London at 6d. a pound.[26]

It was a good thing that the quality of jam had improved, since for many women working in the factories, tea with bread and jam made up a significant part of their daily sustenance. The First World War had a major impact on the fresh berry industry, as farmers were now encouraged in a reverse of policy to replace 'luxury crops' with staples like corn. In Britain, the strawberry acreage fell by 40 per cent, drastically reducing jam supplies. One authority bemoaned this loss, insisting jams were necessary to a population, 'which, full of a steadfast fortitude in the face of military misfortune, was ominously losing its sweetness of disposition owing to the absence of jam and the dubiousness of the supply and quality of margarine'.[27]

The Second World War also had an impact on jam production. When field and factory production switched to wartime footing, the British and American governments turned to those who had always laboured over a hot stove. Women were not only called into the fields to pick fruit in the Women's Land Army, but were asked to 'put down' the fruits of the harvest. In Britain between 1940 and 1945, the Women's Institute preserved over 5,300 tonnes of fruit, the equivalent of a year's jam ration for more than half a million Britons.[28]

By the end of the nineteenth century, jam manufacturing had been established in Canada (E. D. Smith), the United States (J. M. Smucker) and Switzerland (Hero). Surprisingly (or perhaps unsurprisingly) for a country so renowned for its *confiserie*, the French were

Thurbers' fruit
preserves and
jellies, advertising
card, 1870–1900,
Forbes Co., Boston
and New York.

somewhat late into the industrial jam market. Félix Potin, originally
a grocer by profession, built a factory in La Villette in 1869 to process fruits and vegetables for sale in Paris. The business expanded
into two more factories by the 1880s and dozens of stores, creating
a food processing and retail empire of which fruit preserves, packed
into white ceramic jars sporting the Potin trademark, were a small
part. By the 1930s, however, British jams, made with fruits such as
strawberries imported from France, began to dominate the French
market. A regional speciality, such as Bar-le-Duc jelly, produced by
small firms in the Meuse, was produced chiefly for export. It involved
the incredibly time-consuming process of extracting the seeds from

black currants, which was undertaken by trained workers, mainly women, who took the berries home to remove their tiny seeds with the aid of a quill, a model of combined factory and in-home labour also used in other industries. Sugar rationing in the Second World War inspired the founder of St Dalfour to sweeten jams with grape must left over from winemaking, though the company using this family recipe was not founded until 1984. Bonne Maman, with its evocation of artisanal production in a gingham-topped jar with 'handwritten' labels (*'couvercle d'après le motif vichy, et étiquette blanche avec calligraphie comme à la plume'*) was established in 1971 to counterfeit the homemade jam produced by generations of *femmes de ménage*, who had put down their wooden spoons and copper pots and left the kitchen for other pursuits.[29]

A Natural Pharmacopeia

When it comes to berries, Thoreau is never at a loss for words. He insisted not only on 'Nature's bottling', but on her prescriptions:

> We require just so much acid as the cranberries afford in the spring. No tarts that I ever tasted at any table possessed such a refreshing, cheering, encouraging acid that literally put the heart in you and set you on edge for this world's experiences, bracing the spirit, as the cranberries I have plucked in the meadows in the spring. They cut the winters phlegm, and now you can swallow another year of this world without other sauce.[30]

Despite Thoreau's recommendation, fresh berries had, for a long time, a somewhat mixed reputation as being neither good nor healthy to eat. Strawberries were too watery, cloudberries (now known as 'Northern Gold') considered harsh and unpleasant, the *madroño* fruit and blackberries caused headaches, and wortleberries were offensive to the stomach, or so said the herbalist John Gerard. Gerard's massive

Herball, first published in 1597, was the unacknowledged translation of an earlier work by Flemish physician and botanist Rembert Dodoens, and both men made ample reference to classical authors such as Galen, Theophrastus, Dioscorides and Pliny, as well as the works of contemporary botanists and nurserymen such as Matthias de l'Obel, Charles de l'Écluse and John Tradescant. Gerard's *Herball* described hundreds of plants, where and how they grew, when they flowered, and their 'Temperature', uses and virtues. Reading a sixteenth-century herbal is a reminder of all the ills that flesh is heir to, and all the remedies tried, tested or hoped for that physicians attempted.

Berries had their place among the preparations of the herb women and apothecaries. The fruits were used fresh, distilled, dried in the sun, or mixed with honey or sugar and made into conserves and pastes, while leaves, bark and roots were steeped, powdered and boiled into teas. Ascribing to the theory of the four humours, the herbalist assigned a temperature to all parts of the plant. In strawberries, for example, 'The leaves and roots do coole and dry, with an astriction or binding quality: but the berries be cold and moist.' Thus, 'The leaves boyled and applied in manner of a pultis [poultice] taketh away the burning heate in wounds'. The berries, on the other hand, being wet and cool, 'quench thirst, and do allaw [allay] the inflammation or heate of the stomacke', while distilled strawberry juice 'drunke with white Wine is good against the passion of the heart, reviving the spirits, and making the heart merry'. It was also good for scouring the face to take away spots, and for kidney stones.[31] Myrtill or myrtle berries mixed with leek seeds 'stop the spitting of bloude which hath contin-ued a long time'.[32] The herbalist also praised the much-maligned bramble. They 'heale the eies that hang out, hard knots in the funda-ment, and stay the hemorrhoides, if the leaves be laid thereunto'. Moreover,

The leaves of the Bramble boyled in water, with honey, allum, and a little white wine added thereto, make a most excellent lotion or washing water to heale the sores in the mouth, the privie parts of man or woman, and the same decoction fastneth the teeth.[33]

Leaves and berries could cool a fever, cure the bloody flux of cholera, reduce inflammations of the mouth and gums, soothe swollen tonsils, purge the belly, drive out worms, stay vomiting, restore the appetite and cure the toothache. They provided remedy for St Anthony's fire (erysipelas), provoked the urine and drove forth the stone and gravel from the kidneys.

The tradition of herbal remedies continued even as other cures – chemical and mineral – came to the fore. Gerard had described a syrup that the apothecaries called 'Rob', made from black wortleberries which were boiled until thick with honey and sugar; it was still being recommended for 'inflammatory sore throats' more than three hundred years later by Maud Grieve in A Modern Herbal.[34] Grieve, who raised medicinal plants in her nursery in England during the First World War when imported medicinal plants were in short supply, published her own Herbal in 1931. The black currant Rob she described could also be shaped into lozenges (which continue to be popular for sore throats, though cassis might also be a remedy of sorts). Grieve also recommended an application of red currant jelly for blisters and burns, raspberry leaf tea for sore mouth and cankers, and strawberries for rheumatic gout, a remedy commended by no less a botanist and sufferer than Linnaeus. Having been restored to health after a severe attack by eating strawberries, he thereafter ate as many each summer as his stomach could hold.[35] A Modern Herbal devotes many pages to elder, beloved of the fairies and called 'the medicine chest of the country people'. Apparently 'the great Dutch physician Boerhaave never passed an elder without raising his hat, so great an opinion had he of its curative properties.' Grieve also quotes the diarist John Evelyn, who maintained that, 'If the medicinal properties of its leaves, bark and berries were fully known, I cannot tell what our countryman could ail for which he might not fetch a remedy from every hedge, either for sickness, or wounds.'[36]

While Grieve may have advocated hedgerow remedies, others were less certain of the benefits of fresh berries. Overindulgence in blackberries was cited as the cause of 'Scald-head' in children (likely ringworm or any number of other skin eruptions most visible on the uncovered heads of the young). Strawberries too caused strawberry rash, and in one dire case, the *New York Herald* reported that in the summer of 1915, thousands of people in Connecticut suffered from 'intense itching, and some persons, unable to sleep or to obtain relief, have become temporarily insane'. Despite Linnaeus' claims of strawberry consumption as a cure for gout, these strawberry eaters were also afflicted with rheumatic pains so severe that 'Several persons thought they had suffered a paralytic stroke.'[37] Perhaps even worse, across the Atlantic it was reported that ladies who ate too many strawberries became 'sulky and irritable':

> Some of them will eat a pound or more of strawberries at a time and then become so morose that people are glad to avoid them . . . They are suffering from the strawberry disease, the symptoms of which are slight dizziness, a desire to be alone and intolerance of being questioned.

The remedy was limiting maximum strawberry consumption to a pottle of twelve.[38] Jacob Biggle, the eponymous author of *The Biggle Berry Book* (1911), insisted, however, that for some young women, strawberries were the best medicine: 'A very intelligent young lady living opposite my farm, who has travelled the world over, enjoys life just as long as the supply of berries continues; but at other seasons she is more or less of an invalid.' He also cited Amos Root, a celebrated nineteenth-century American beekeeper and author, who praised the health benefits of berries:

> Everybody ought to have all the strawberries they want. If they do not care to grow them they ought to be in some business so that they can afford to buy them quart after

quart, morning, noon and night. Not only because they give enjoyment but because they are the cheapest, best and most natural medicine to tone up the system that has ever been invented. They are both victuals and drink. The man who cannot afford to give up his beer, tea and coffee, yes, and tobacco too, when strawberries are plenty and cheap, is a man to be pitied.[39]

By the beginning of the twentieth century, physicians, chemists and herbalists like Maud Grieve were seeking to understand the properties that caused some berries to be baleful and others beneficial. The observation of effects in patients, and a review of medical literature as well as folk remedies, began to contribute to a more scientific understanding of the health benefits of eating berries, or their various preparations, from syrups to pastilles and powders. (I have sweet childhood memories of black currant lozenges and drafts of Ribena.) According to an interview in 1907 with vegetarian tennis player Eustace Miles, who may have indulged in too many strawberries at Wimbledon, any disorders from overindulgence were associated with eating unripe strawberries, which contained three

The 'Allenburys' Glycerine and Black Currant Pastilles.

Sarah Miriam Peale, *Basket of Berries*, 1860, oil on canvas.

different acids – phosphoric, sulphuric and silicic, the latter being the cause of digestive grief. Fruit acids could also be healing, and Grieve noted that elderberries were useful in treating bronchitis and similar 'troubles' because they contained viburnic acid, which induces perspiration.[40]

Berries do, in fact, contain a high proportion of phenolic acids, one of the many phytochemicals that help protect the plants themselves against bacterial and fungal infections, ultraviolet radiation and other hazards. As chemists and physicians experimented with botanical extracts, they began to realize the complexity of their bio-chemistry and the difficulty of isolating the action of any particular agent. By the First World War, international research on deficiency diseases such as beriberi, scurvy and rickets revealed unknown sub-stances essential to good health, which scientists named 'vitamines' – a contraction of 'vital amines'. These appeared most abundant, like minerals, in the outer coverings and the germ of grains, and in fruits and vegetables. The once neglected 'watery fruits and vegetables' were now recommended as part of a more balanced diet. Better still for the emerging weight loss industry, they contained few calories.

Ongoing research into vitamins (Vitamin C was named in 1919) reinforced the public perception that fresh fruits, including berries, were good for you. In the 1950s scientists started to explore phyto-nutrients in many foods; by the 1980s they began to identify chemicals in plants with antioxidant, anti-inflammatory and antimicrobial effects that might be used to fight diseases such as arthritis and cancer, or heart attack and stroke. Not only were berries a good-for-you diet

Dried elderberries (*Sambucus*).

food, they were now classified as one of the new 'functional foods' that were not just nourishment but could claim health benefits based on scientific research. This approach to the traditional berry remedies of the herbalists has opened a floodgate of new research. One avenue has focused on the flavonoid anthocyanin that causes the deep colours of berries and acts as a powerful antioxidant. The blacker the berry, the richer in anthocyanin; for example, a single 100-gram (3½ oz) serving of black currant can provide up to 750 milligrams of anthocyanin, which research has suggested would have a significant therapeutic effect on vision.[41]

Berries have other useful properties; researchers have confirmed that cranberries, long used as a folk remedy for urinary tract infections, have important antibacterial properties.[42] Berries also have anti-inflammatory qualities, vindicating Linnaeus' advocacy of strawberries as a possible remedy for gout. Other berries may have potential for treatment of cardiovascular disease, Alzheimer's disease and Type 2 diabetes. While observational studies suggest that berries do indeed hold promise for public health, their functionality and long-term impacts have not been thoroughly studied, the breathless pronouncements of the international berry associations and modern-day herbalists, naturopaths and health-food purveyors – berries are 'superfoods', 'better than drugs' – to the contrary.[43] As one nutritionist put it, 'The preventive effects of fruits and vegetables cannot be explained by just one phytonutrient that is taken out of the context of a healthy diet.' She suggested that eating a wide variety of fruits and vegetables was the best strategy, and that the world would undoubtedly be a poorer place if we reduced our eating of the sweet fruits of the earth to purely functional values. After all, she said, quoting Thoreau, 'The value of those wild fruits is not in the mere possession or eating of them, but in the sight and enjoyment of them.'[44]

six
The Global Berry

ealthy, slimming, delicious and exotic, berries are on everyone's menu and in their shopping carts worldwide. The fragile productions of country lanes or open fields are now part of the global fruit market, grown under plastic, on table-tops and in substrate, fumigated, chilled and shipped year-round. When George Darrow wrote his definitive work on the strawberry in 1965, he estimated world acreage to be 'probably between 300,000 and 400,000 acres [120,000 and 160,000 ha], of which about 130,000 [52,500 ha] are in North America, 20,000 in Japan, and the rest mostly in Europe.'[1] Just over fifty years later, the acreage devoted to strawberries worldwide has almost tripled, and strawberry fields cover the ground not only in North America but in China, Mexico, Spain, Turkey, Korea, Egypt and Poland.[2]

Berries are big business and the business is growing exponentially in the twenty-first century. Since 1961 the United Nations Food and Agriculture Organization (FAO) has been tracking global production for a large variety of crops, including berries. FAO has gathered data on the acreage, yields and harvests of strawberries, blueberries, gooseberries, currants and raspberries, as well as cranberries and kiwis. The strawberry remains far and away the most beloved berry on a global scale. In 2017 world production was more than 9 million tonnes; of the traditional soft fruits, including blueberries, cranberries, currants and gooseberries, only raspberries (at 812,000 tonnes) even approached 1 million tonnes on the market. While 9 million tonnes

Trendy smoothie bowl with fresh fruit, avocado, chia seeds and berries.

is an impressive number, it was only just over 1 per cent of world fruit production, dwarfed by the giants of the global fruit market – watermelons, bananas, apples, oranges and grapes.[3] The FAO admits that it does not capture all the wild harvested fruits (and that most certainly applies to berries), but does present the big picture. What is even more revealing is to look at the changes in global harvests over the last fifty years. With the exception of grapes, where production has grown by only a modest 80 per cent, apples, oranges and pineapples have shown phenomenal growth, and in most cases, production has more than quintupled. Strawberries may not be the largest segment of global fruit production, but over the half-century since 1961, the world is growing twelve times more strawberries.

What accounts for this startling rise in global production? There are certainly more of us, and we are eating more fruit. Historically, the Americans and British have been the great berry consumers. After the Second World War, when fresh fruits were once again being harvested and sold, American families ate an average of just under 5.4 kilograms (12 lb) per week, and berries accounted for slightly over 225 grams (8 oz) of that; they were also eating their blueberries, raspberries and cranberries from cans.[4] Seventy years later, in 2015, they consumed over 4.5 kilograms (10 lb) of fresh berries per capita per year, and that was double the amount they were eating in 2000.[5] While strawberries continued to dominate the berry basket (on average, an American eats 3.6 kilograms (8 lb) per year), in the twenty years from 1994 to 2014, blueberry consumption also grew by almost 600 per cent.[6] In the United Kingdom in 1948, an individual ate, on average, less

A wheel-chart showing foods to be combined in a balanced diet. No 'berries' are pictured. U.S. Department of Agriculture, 1943, colour lithograph.

Strawberries at a supermarket in Hong Kong, 2014.

than a pound or 450 grams of any fruit per week. Fruit consumption has been rising since 2000, and berries have outstripped apples and bananas as the largest fresh fruit category on British tables.[7] The soft fruits now make up almost a quarter of all fresh fruit sold in the UK and over the last twenty years, the British have more than doubled their intake of strawberries and raspberries, for which they have a particular passion.[8]

But it is not only these berry-loving nations that are driving demand. China is the dark horse of berry consumption. Numerous varieties of strawberries are native to China's vast forests and fields and have formed part of the traditional pharmacopeia. Today the Middle Kingdom is the world's largest producer of strawberries (twice the production of the United States) and its greatest consumer (41 per cent of world consumption). Now blueberries are also becoming part of the Chinese diet, and while current consumption is minuscule compared to the quantities eaten by blueberry-loving Americans, imports from the United States, Canada and Chile have grown by a factor of twelve in recent years, and demand continues to increase, particularly among younger, affluent shoppers.[9] The strawberry in China is associated with innocence and sweetness, and is now used with some irony to describe those born after 1990. The 'Strawberry Generation' never had to 'eat bitterness' or endure the hardships of their parents and grandparents; they are sweet and innocent and soft. In Taiwan, however, the much-criticized members of the Strawberry Generation wear their berry labels with pride – young politically active Taiwanese now self-identify as 'Wild Strawberries' and 'Little Blueberries', no longer so innocent and far less sweet.[10]

Extending the Season

Much of this incremental growth in berry production is the result of a demand for fresh berries. While a substantial part of the berry harvest still goes to processing for preserves or juice, and increasingly to deep-freezing, fresh consumption is driving the market. Fresh berries are delicious, healthy, convenient and now readily available on supermarket shelves. Traditionally, the amount of fresh berries that could be consumed for either pleasure or health was limited by availability. Until the early twentieth century, most berry lovers had to be content with eating fresh what they could for a few weeks, and then putting the fruit down to be enjoyed later in another guise. Growers were, of course, not content with such a

Plastic greenhouses covering 20,000 ha of the Campo de Dalías, southwest of Almería in southern Spain, seen from space, 2004.

short season. They sought varieties that would fruit earlier, last longer and produce prolifically. Breeders happily complied, and the profusion of varieties and cultivars in the nineteenth and early twentieth centuries is evidence of both the plants' abilities to adapt to different soils and growing conditions, and the dedication of the horticulturalists, who sought optimal characteristics combining early or late fruiting, flavour, size and durability. But even modern berries need a little help to produce fruit in and out of season. The gardeners of Versailles could extend the brief season by growing the royal strawberries under glass, truly finding strawberries in winter fit for a Sun King. In the 1960s growers in the United Kingdom adopted a modern version of the gardener's glasshouse – the polytunnel. Where fields of strawberries once dreamed under a summer sun, now almost all British strawberries bask under plastic. Polytunnels extend the local growing season to 26 weeks and increase yields by a third, though to the consternation of some country dwellers, they have changed the appearance of strawberry fields forever.[11] Low tunnels are now also a common sight in North America, Asia and Europe, as are high tunnels for blackberries, blueberries and raspberries, which cover hectares of ground with Gothic arches of glistening polyethylene film.[12] Mulching has also been an important part of berry cultivation, retaining moisture and suppressing weeds. Plastic 'mulch' originated in California and Florida in the 1960s, replacing straw and sawdust with long sheets of shiny black polyethylene. In the last three decades, China has covered vast amounts of land with plastic mulch to conserve water and improve yields for its berry crops. Plastic mulch allows growers to plant earlier, control weeds and pests, and produce more, larger and cleaner berries. Plasticulture now dominates commercial cultivation worldwide, contributing to the increase in global production of plastic as well as local pollution.[13]

Despite growers' best efforts to protect and nourish their crops, berry cultivation can still be hampered by poor growing seasons and an abundance of pests, most of which live in the unhygienic earth. It is somewhat of a miracle that we eat any berries at all, given the pests that bedevil them, from grey mould ('a silent strawberry nemesis'[14]) and leaf and cane rust, to the dreaded mummy berry that

Blueberry bush infected by Blueberry Shock Virus, 2012.

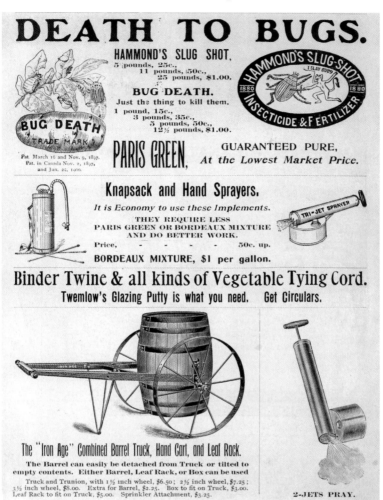

'Death to Bugs', in *Bolgiano's 1902 Catalogue: Tested Seeds for the Garden and Farm*, Washington, DC.

afflicts blueberries, and the direly named anthracnose. And these are only some of the fungi. Jacob Biggle fought them all, and in his book about berries that provided 'Small Fruit Facts from Bud to Box Conserved into Understandable Form', he enumerated crown-borers, leaf-rollers, white grubs and root lice, cane-borers, gall-beetles, tree crickets and sawflies, not to mention sucking insects like aphids. For

'Horticulturist
Fumiomi Takeda
of the Applachian
Fruit Reseach Station
in West Virginia
inspects the size
and quality of
hydroponically grown
strawberries, 1998'.

each of these, there were traditional remedies, from the relatively benign practice of mowing and burning after fruiting, to almost constant spraying with fungicides such as 'Bordeaux mixture' (copper sulphate and quicklime) and powdered sulphur, as well as insecticides that included Paris green (a highly toxic inorganic compound), arsenate of lead and kerosene or whale oil emulsions. Bordeaux mixture is still being used today, and growers have added to their arsenal compounds such as methyl bromide (not only toxic but recently banned as an ozone-depleting substance) and dimethoate (a broad-spectrum organophosphate, a toxic substance also used in nerve agents, and one of the most common causes of agricultural poisoning worldwide). Crops grown in the United States are tested for pesticide residues by the Department of Agriculture and the Food and Drug Administration, and each year the non-profit Environmental Working Group (EWG) combs through the most recent reports to rank the 'Dirty Dozen'; in 2018 strawberries were number one.[15] While the USDA assures consumers that washing in tap water rinses away any harmful amounts of the 22 different residues left on some strawberries from these chemical baths, fruit lovers are becoming decidedly reluctant to ingest toxins. Organic fruits are increasing in market share,[16] and even conventional growers are using new organic or biopesticides and changing their practices, mulching with 'VIF and TIF' (virtually and totally impermeable films) – the next generation of plasticulture products that retain and prolong the effects of reduced doses of pesticides.[17]

The ultimate solution, however, seems to require removing the plants from any contact with pest-ridden soil. Francis Bacon, the great seventeenth-century empiricist, experimented with growing plants in water and averred that 'for nourishment the Water is almost all in all, and that the Earth doth but keep the Plant upright'.[18] Strawberries are particularly suited to soilless cultivation, and commercial substrate

A greenhouse designed for *Ichigo-gari* ('strawberry picking'), Japan, 2008.

growing systems were first developed in the early 1970s in greenhouses in the Netherlands and Belgium. The use of these systems enabled year-round strawberry production and avoided the vicissitudes of root diseases, nematodes and insects. Bacon added 'horse-dung' to his water to improve growth, and modern growers add a nutrient soup to the troughs of well-watered substrates of peat, coconut fibre (coir) or perlite. Due to their shallow root structures, strawberries can also be grown on the thin nutrient films developed by a Japanese researcher in the 1990s. Made of hydrogel – a super-absorbent material (used, for example, in sanitary products) – these polymer films can be laid across any flat surface and provide everything a growing strawberry needs, resulting in increased yields of very clean berries; though, as one journalist wondered, do we really need 'cling wrap' fields?[19] Soilless growing also means no more stooping to ground level. Strawberries can be plucked at tabletop height, easing the backs of the armies of commercial pickers and also encouraging twenty-first-century 'pick your own' operations. While a day out strawberry picking was once associated with farmers' fields, buzzing bees and dirty knees, day-trippers now flock to bright greenhouses with rows of tables full of strawberry plants, the berries clean, ripe and ready to eat.

Strawberry Specials and Blueberry Boats

Even the best cultivation practices cannot extend the growing season indefinitely. For truly year-round availability, most countries have to import their berries, at least for part of the year. Historically, shipping soft fruits long distances was a risky business. The refrigerated box-cars of the 'Strawberry Specials' that raced from California to the eastern seaboard of the United States in the dark days of late winter had high rates of spoilage. Apples, oranges and bananas – the champions of the fresh fruit market – were robust enough to withstand days of travel across country or weeks at sea. Few berries, other than the barrels of American cranberries that sailed across the ocean to Britain, could make such long voyages. Frozen berries became a

'Reefer' or mechanical refrigeration car, built by Pacific Fruit Express Company, late 1950s. Photograph taken in 2018.

mainstay of the global shipping trade, but the rising consumer demand for fresh fruit has changed the way berries are packaged, shipped and sold. The worldwide trade in fresh berries has grown exponentially since the early 2000s, and the chief exporting countries have increased their production and expanded into new territories to keep up with what is now year-round demand. Americans eat all the strawberries they grow, so that one of the world's largest berry businesses, Driscoll's, a family enterprise that began in California in the 1860s, now 'follows the sun and Mother Nature' to supply the North American and the galloping Chinese markets, with farms in Florida, Mexico and Australia. Americans cannot grow enough blueberries, raspberries and blackberries to meet their own appetites, so that they import blueberries from Canada and Chile – home to many native *Vaccinium* species – as well as from Argentina, Mexico and, increasingly, Peru, and all their blackberries come from Mexico. The plastic greenhouse seas of Spain and new production facilities in Morocco slake the berry hunger of the United Kingdom and the European Union. China itself exports berries, as does South Africa, and when it comes to the kiwi, New Zealand leads the pack.

Rows of heavily fruiting kiwifruit plants in an orchard, New Zealand, 2014.

While most of the growth in berry cultivation has been in the traditional top four – strawberries, blueberries, raspberries and cranberries (with blackberries rambling up the rear) – kiwis (*Actinidia* sp.) appeared out of nowhere in the 1970s to compete with strawberries in quantity as a global fruit.[20] Also known as the Chinese gooseberry, the fruit is native to north-central and eastern China, where it grows prolifically. The Chinese called it 'monkey peach' (*yang tao*), since the monkeys also enjoyed it, and it is used in traditional medicines. In 1904 the Chinese gooseberry was imported into New Zealand, and by 1930 was in commercial production. In 1959, when exports to North America began, it was renamed 'kiwifruit' after New Zealand's famous flightless bird, the kiwi – also a nickname for New Zealanders.[21] China today produces half of global production, but New Zealand and Italy are the top exporters of the golden- and green-fleshed fuzzy berries.

The huge volumes of soft fruit circling the globe demand improved transport methods. Straw punnets and wooden veneer strawberry baskets cannot withstand the rigours of long-distance shipping (though they are still attractive for local retailers and pick-your-own operations with a vintage theme). Plastics once again provide a solution. In the 1990s Driscoll's introduced a clear plastic clamshell, and in 2015 estimated that their workers packed berries into 1.2 billion of them. The clamshells are placed into crates, stacked on pallets and cooled down before being loaded into chilled containers, to be shipped by air, land or sea. 'Cool chain management' is critical to shipping success. Blueberries, for example, are cooled to just above freezing, where they must remain for the entire length of their voyage. If the temperature of the container falls too low, the berries freeze and burst their skins; if too high, they continue their natural post-harvest life cycle, giving off carbon dioxide, ripening, decaying and fermenting. Growers attempt to mitigate the difficulties of ensuring continuous cooling by reducing travel time, and most South American blueberries are shipped by air. But cooling is not enough to guarantee that berries arrive sweet and sound at market. Joining the berries on their global rounds are the flies, beetles, worms and fungi they have grown up with. Different jurisdictions demand different treatments to ensure these stowaways do not become naturalized at their destination, so that the majority of berries, with the exception of those labelled organic, are fumigated in containers prior to shipping, or more recently, irradiated.[22] Once the berries arrive at their destination, sprayed, cooled and attractively packaged, they have a very limited shelf life. Picked from their bushes or canes, berries do not cease their active metabolic life. They continue to breathe, and in their respiration lies the beginning of decay. Blackberries and raspberries, the great breathers of the berry world, start to spoil within two to five days; cranberries are champions of long-term storage and last months, while blueberries have a shelf life of only one or two weeks.[23] The customer judges berries chiefly by eye, peering through the lid of a clamshell. Are they ripe and juicy? Are there any mouldy ones? And are they deep red, blue or purple . . .?

Superfruits

In 2005 the first International Berry Health Benefits Symposium brought together a multidisciplinary group of international participants from Asia, Europe, New Zealand, Mexico and North and South America, including growers and packers, scientists, dieticians and health-care workers. They met to share research on berries as 'functional foods', rich in antioxidants and other health-giving nutrients with difficult-to-pronounce names, such as anthocyanin, polyphenols and flavonoids. Up until the 1990s, the number of papers published annually on anthocyanin in the biomedical literature could be counted in the dozens; after 2000 it was in the hundreds. Research in functional foods followed a similar trajectory, beginning a few years earlier, and by the mid-2000s comprising thousands of studies each year.[24] Research into botanicals is hardly new, and many drugs in the contemporary medical arsenal have been derived from phytochemicals. What is new is the idea that diets rich in certain foods can effectively prevent or even cure common maladies.

This research interest has translated into the popular health and nutrition literature as the search for 'superfoods'. 'Superfood' is not a technical term, though in deference to its widespread use, the *Oxford English Living Dictionary* defines it as 'A nutrient-rich food considered to be especially beneficial for health and well-being.'[25] 'Superfruit' was added to the lexicon in 2004, and the deep, dark, delicious polyphenol-rich berries were star players. The darker the berry, the more anthocyanin, and presumably the greater the health benefits. Blueberries certainly profited from being classed as a superfood, and their popularity soared from the mid-2000s. Since 2006, fresh blueberry consumption has more than quadrupled in the UK, not a historic market, and the little blues are increasingly part of a healthy diet for British households.[26] Most research on berry benefits has been conducted in laboratories testing high concentrations of the phytochemicals, using in-vitro methods or experimental animals (rats crammed with berries). Eating enough fresh berries to get the predicted results might be challenging for most people, and the berries richest in antioxidant, disease-fighting polyphenols are not necessarily the easiest eating. Strawberries show poorly, raspberries middling, raw blackberries thankfully are stars, but raw black currants and raw elderberries, not usually eaten by the handful without a good deal of sweetening, score very high. Worse still, it seems that the bioavailability of many compounds is affected not only by how they are grown and processed, but by the actions of our own digestion.[27]

These findings have not, however, impeded the promotion of the next generation of exotic berry superfruits. Strawberries, blackberries and cranberries may be good for you, but these novel fruits are seemingly better, rarer and more expensive. In the mid-2000s, several new berries appeared in the global berry markets. None were actually new, and most had been eaten or ingested for millennia in various parts of the world, but with the increasing importance of diet as cure, they were praised and sold as effective functional foods. Goji berry (*Lycium barbarum*, also known as wolfberry) is grown primarily in China, where it has been long used in herbal medicine. A member of the much-reviled and praised nightshade (Solanaceae) family (sunberries, tomatoes, ground cherries), the berries are eaten raw or used in teas and soups in China; as export products, they are often incorporated for their health benefits in granola bars, salads, 'smoothies' and juice.[28] Sea buckthorn (*Hippophae* species) is another 'berry' now imported from China, though it grows extensively in northern Europe, Russia and Canada. Rather unpleasant raw, it requires 'bletting' or frosting to bring out its flavour, but it too has become a popular juice, apparently good for gastrointestinal problems. Haskap berries are strangely shaped and deep-blue – a sign of good flavonoids – and are the fruit of the deep-blue honeysuckle (*Lonicera caerulea*), known in Canada by the prosaic name 'Swamp fly honeysuckle' but marketed as 'Polar Jewel'. The name 'haskap' is derived from an Ainu word, and while Japan remains an important consumer market, Canada has taken to growing the native haskaps, selling them dried, in jam and in a flavoured mead. The European Food Safety Authority (EFSA) has recently agreed that

Wolfberries ('goji'. *Lycium barbarum*). Zhongning. Ningxia. China. 2005.

haskap is indeed an edible berry and can be sold in the European Union, but it does not endorse benefits other than edibility. The haskap would certainly seem unable to compete with the claims of another native Canadian superfruit, the saskatoon berry (*Amelanchier alnifolia*), 'the purple berry packing a healthy punch!' This fruit, actually a small apple-like pome, was traditionally used by Indigenous people in pemmican and by settlers in pies and jams, but is now touted as 'super fruit packed full of PurpleFuel'. This delicious berry is a great source of calcium, fibre, iron, manganese, magnesium, phytosterols, phenolics, anthocyanins and vitamin E – to name a few![29]

The days when berries were marketed for flavour, size and delectable appearance (difficult to promote in the case of saskatoon berries) have passed, and selling berries now demands an exposition on their antioxidant fighting prowess – 'saskatoons have a higher potential to neutralize free radicals than blueberries' – or their contribution to battling the demon of the West, cholesterol – 'plant sterols help reduce the cholesterol levels in moderately to highly cholesterolemic adults'. All claims are supported by reference to scientific research, citing articles from *Current Molecular Medicine*, *Phytochemistry*, the *Journal of Nutrition*, the *Journal of Urology* and laboratory tests, making one long for the days when berries were marketed simply as delicious.[30] Açai berries, promoted with equal enthusiasm by advocates – 'the açai berry (*Euterpe oleracea*) is one of the most nutritious berries on the planet' – are not even berries.[31] The açai palm, native to South America, produces large quantities of dark-coloured drupes, which have been a dietary staple in the Amazon basin for centuries. It was their flamboyant marketing in North America in the 2000s that forced researchers to test the fruit against other miracle berries and determine that, while certainly a nutritious fruit, the coveted antioxidant capacity was less than a glass of blueberry juice or red wine.[32]

Not all exotic berries are becoming better known and more widely available outside their native habitats. Surely there should be a market for the giant Colombian blackberry, the *zarzamora*? *Rubus macrocarpus* is huge in comparison to your average blackberry, almost too large to be eaten in one mouthful, but unfortunately proving difficult to grow outside its narrow range high in the Colombian Andes. Growers might have better luck with the *mortiño* (*Vaccinium floribundum*), known in Ecuador as 'grapes of the moor' or 'fruits of desire'. The *mortiño* grows wild in the Andes, where it has been collected for use in traditional medicine, but is also enjoyed in jams and as a kind of morbid smoothie, *colada morada*, made for the Day of the Dead in November. According to an anthropologist, the dark-purple drink symbolizes the blood of the llamas and people once sacrificed in religious practices.[33] And what about *lulo*, which makes a delicious iced drink sold in roadside cafes in Ecuador and Colombia? Also called the *naranjilla* or little orange, *Solanum quitoense* is a member of the family that brought us the tomato, and was eaten by the Incas. Despite being prolific and tasty, it has not become a superfruit, perhaps because it is orange? And there is the antipodean wonder, the bush tomato (*Solanum centrale*), also known as *kutjera*, *kampurarpa* or *akatjura* among Aboriginal peoples in central Australia. It is similar in flavour to sun-dried tomato, and like strawberries, the fruit is very fragrant; when ripe, it perfumes the air of the outback with a sweet caramel aroma.[34] On the damp slopes of the northwest coast of North America, home to so many small fruits, grows the salal (*Gaultheria shallon*), eaten for millennia by the Haida and other nations but now used commercially in floral arrangements. Recent research has, however, promoted it as a 'contender for the title of healthiest berry', so that floral use

Solanum centrale, Royal Botanic Gardens Cranbourne, Victoria, Australia, 2013.

may soon be superseded by culinary.[35] Most of these fruits are picked wild or on small farms, their processing artisanal, consumption local and research into their properties limited. Perhaps those who gather and eat them experience the same earthy joys that Thoreau felt when he picked the wild huckleberry. Once targeted and moved to the clingfilm of greenhouse nutrient culture, their production and availability may soar, but something might also be lost in these tastes of the earth.

Our desire for tiny sweet fruits whenever and wherever we are ('People just have to have their blueberries'[36]) has propelled a global industry with what appears to be a very heavy reliance on plasticulture, pesticides, fertilizers, irrigation and chiefly female migrant labour. The plastic seas of polyethylene, the hydrogel film of tabletop cultivation, and the toxic cocktails of chemicals that protect and nurture the delicate berries, have made frolicsome berry-picking in open fields a romantic fable. Innocence and desire still drive the market, but it is increasingly difficult to cast the jet-setting, overbred and artificially nurtured berry as one of the sweet pleasures of a simpler way of life. The berry crop is, of course, only a small part of the global fruit trade, dominated by bananas, oranges and apples, and even their volumes are dwarfed by the world market for cereals and oils. What is obvious, despite the rising demand for organic produce and new technologies to reduce use of agricultural chemicals, is that our clean, stemmed berries, nestled into sparkling clamshells like Aurora in her crystal coffin, are the products of an industrialized agriculture, so far removed from nature that we may well have to classify them as manufactured goods. These fruits of the clingwrap fields would horrify Thoreau, who eschewed even purchasing his wild, sweet berries. Picking them in the fields was not just half the fun, it was the whole of it:

> It is a grand fact that you cannot make the fairer fruits or parts of fruits matter of commerce; that is, you cannot buy the highest use and enjoyment of them. You cannot buy that pleasure which it yields to him who truly plucks it. You

cannot buy a good appetite, even. In short, you may buy a servant or slave, but you cannot buy a friend.[37]

We befriended berries long ago and welcomed them as food of the gods. We may be called upon to rethink our insatiable desires if we want to maintain our innocent relationship with the ephemeral and intoxicating soft fruits of the earth.

Timeline

50,000–30,000 years BP	Migrating birds distribute crowberries between polar regions
1275	Edward I imports gooseberries from Normandy
1368	Jean Dudoy, the royal gardener, plants strawberries for Charles V at the Louvre
1536	Antonius Musa Brassavola records he has safely enjoyed eggplant, as cooked by two ladies of Spain
1557	Spanish-Incan historian Garcilaso de la Vega describes a fruit named the *chili* (the South American strawberry) as 'of excellent taste and very good to eat'
1570	Bartolomeo Scappi, chef to popes and princes and author of *Opera dell'arte del cucinare*, suggests strawberries be added to a goat's milk pudding in spring
1610	Samuel de Champlain, the founder of Quebec, samples a snowberry (*Gaultheria hispidula*)
1643	Roger Williams, in his account of New England, says that natives dry the whortleberry and 'beat to powder and mingle it with their parched meal, and make a delicate dish which they call Sautauthig'
1692	François Massialot, *chef de cuisine* to innumerable aristocrats, publishes *Nouvelle instruction pour les confitures, les liqueurs, et les fruits*

1714	Amédée François Frézier presents a South American strawberry plant to Antoine de Jussieu 'to cultivate in the King's Garden'
1740	The first Gooseberry Club is founded in Lancashire, England
1747	Hannah Glasse makes Gooseberry fool
1750	Carolus Linnaeus, the father of taxonomy, cures his gout by eating wood strawberries
1751	Carolus Linnaeus defines a berry in *Philosophia botanica*
1764	Nineteen-year-old Antoine Nicolas Duchesne, protégé of the royal botanist Bernard de Jussieu, presents Louis XIV with a splendid example of *Fragaria chiloensis* – the South American strawberry – bearing enormous fruits
1806	French *confiseur* Nicolas Appert develops the process of bottling fruits and vegetables by sealing them tightly and immersing them in boiling water
1810	Henry Hall, a farmer in Cape Cod, Massachusetts, transplants cranberry vines into a drained bog, covers them in sand and harvests a bumper crop
1819	British grower Michael Keens raises a better strawberry from seed, the 'Keens Seedling'
1841	Crosse & Blackwell mass-produce jam
1850	Mrs Bliss shares her recipe for blueberry pie in the *Practical Cook Book*
1851	James Wilson, a Scottish nurseryman living near Albany, New York, breeds the self-pollinating Wilson strawberry
1852	The 'London' gooseberry wins 333 prizes, weighing in at 896 grains, the size of a small apple
1858	John Landis Mason, an American tinsmith, patents the Mason jar

1869	Félix Potin, originally a grocer by profession, builds his factory in La Villette to process fruits and vegetables for Paris
1870	Joseph White publishes *Cranberry Culture*
1881	Judge Logan crosses a raspberry and a blackberry in his garden in Santa Cruz, California, to create the loganberry
1882	Canadian farmer Ernest D'Israeli Smith makes jam from his excess fruit and founds E. D. Smith
1897	J. M. Smucker founds a company to make jams and jellies in Ohio
1904	Driscoll's, the California-based global berry company, is founded as 'Banner Berry Farm's Brand'
1905	Luther Burbank creates the controversial 'Sunberry' (*Solanum villosum* × *S. guineense*)
1910	Two Swiss jam makers, Henckell and Roth, launch the Hero brand
1911	Frederick Coville crosses a highbush with a lowbush plant to create the modern commercial blueberry
1918	Coville and his partner Elizabeth White, the 'Blueberry Queen', sell their first berries
1926	Amateur Louisiana gardener B. M. Young releases the Youngberry
1931	Maud Grieve praises the health benefits of berries in *A Modern Herbal*
1932	Walter Knott first sells boysenberries at a roadside stand
1934	Mrs Knott serves fried chicken and her signature Boysenberry Pies in Knott's Chicken Dinner Restaurant

1959	New Zealand exporters rename the Chinese gooseberry 'kiwifruit'
1960s	Growers in the United Kingdom adopt the polytunnel for berry cultivation
1970s	Dutch and Belgian growers develop soilless berry cultivation
1971	French company Bonne Maman launches a commercial jam with a homemade look
1985	First commercial blueberries are planted in Chile
1990s	Driscoll's introduces the clear plastic clamshell package for fresh berries
1995	Japanese chemical physicist Yuichi Mori founds Mebiol to promote thin-film farming using hydrogel
2000s	'New' superberries – goji, sea buckthorn, haskap – appear in the global berry markets
2004	'Superfruit' is added to the lexicon
2005	The first International Berry Health Benefits Symposium takes place
2006	U.S. Food and Drug Administration (FDA) warns two goji juice distributors against claiming unproven therapeutic benefits
2013	The International Symposium on Superfruits: Myth or Truth? is hosted by the Food and Agricultural Organization of the United Nations (FAO) in Ho Chi Minh City, Vietnam
2018	Britain goes 'berry-mad' and buys more berries than bananas

References
❀

Preface
1 Henry David Thoreau, *Wild Fruits: Thoreau's Rediscovered Last Manuscript*, ed. Bradley P. Dean (New York, 2000), p. 22.
2 Ray Bradbury, *Dandelion Wine* [1957] (Harper Collins e-book, 2008), p. 19.

1 Berries True and False
1 The others were capsula, siliqua, legumen, folliculus, drupa, pomum and strobilis. Later botanists increased the number of types of fruit to 45, and the classification of fruits continues to bedevil botanists. The nineteenth-century botanist Matthias Jacob Schleiden complained in frustration that,

> Nowhere has purely diagrammatic comprehension been so prevalent as in the theory of the fruit, nowhere have botanists starting from the language of common life, and merely multiplying the words, taken so little pains to define with scientific strictness; and hence nowhere does terminology so vacillate among all the definitions as in the fruit. One assumes 10, another 14, a third 20, and another 40 or 60 kinds of fruit, in short, the confusion is indescribable.

Cited in Richard W. Spjut, 'A Systematic Treatment of Fruit Types', *Memoirs of the New York Botanical Garden*, LXX (1994), n.p., www.worldbotanical.com.
2 The golden apples of the West were unlikely, however, to have been oranges, which originated in Asia; ibid.
3 Despite the fruits being the longer-lasting productions of a plant, botanists still use, as Linnaeus did, the structure of their ephemeral flowers to classify the great floral families.
4 Alfred Russel Wallace, 'The Colours of Plants and the Origin of the Colour-sense', in *Tropical Nature and Other Essays* (London, 1878), pp. 221–46, 224–5.

5 H. Martin Schaefer, Alfredo Valido and Pedro Jordano, 'Birds See the True Colours of Fruits to Live off the Fat of the Land', *Proceedings of the Royal Society B: Biological Sciences*, 22 February 2014, DOI: https://doi.org/10.1098/rspb.2013.2516.

6 Magnus Popp, Virginia Mirré and Christian Brochmann, 'A Single Mid-Pleistocene Long-distance Dispersal by a Bird Can Explain the Extreme Bipolar Disjunction in Crowberries (*Empetrum*)', PNAS, CVIII/16, pp. 6, 520–25 (19 April 2011), www.pnas.org.

7 T. H. Fleming and W. John Kress, *The Ornaments of Life: Coevolution and Conservation in the Tropics* (Chicago, IL, 2013), p. 363.

8 The food writer Waverley Root described the effect of the first warm air of spring on a field near his farm:

as I reached my mailbox, still a mile short of the house, I sensed a sudden sweetness in the air . . . the hillside . . . lay actually under a thick carpet of wild strawberries. With the first warm breath of spring they had sprung into bloom, all at once: their fragrance was so strong that I had smelled it a mile away.
Waverley Root, *Food* (New York, 1986), p. 482.

9 Fruits eaten by birds, such as elderberries, rely on visual signals – deep-purple berries with highly visible red stems – to attract their avian consumers. See Omer Nevo et al., 'Fruit Odor as a Ripeness Signal for Seed-dispersing Primates? A Case Study on Four Neotropical Plant Species', *Journal of Chemical Ecology*, XLII (2016), pp. 323–8, www.ncbi.nlm.nih.gov.

10 Robert Dudley, 'Ethanol, Fruit Ripening, and the Historical Origins of Human Alcoholism in Primate Frugivory', *Integrative and Comparative Biology*, XLIV/4 (2004), pp. 315–23. In 2014 Dudley published *The Drunken Monkey: Why We Drink and Abuse Alcohol* (Berkeley, CA, 2014), based on research into other frugivores and ethanol.

11 Jeff Hecht, 'Drunk Birds Had One-too-many Berries to Blame', *New Scientist Daily News*, 25 (May 2012), www.newscientist.com.

12 Henry David Thoreau, *Wild Fruits: Thoreau's Rediscovered Last Manuscript*, ed. Bradley P. Dean (New York, 2000), p. 32.

13 Modern systems of classification have changed a great deal since Linnaeus compared the numbers of stamens and pistils in flowers to create his taxonomies of genus and species. The classifications discussed here are based on the Angiosperm Phylogeny Group (APG) classification updated in 2016. This classification is evidence of new understanding of relationships between plants uncovered through phylogenetic analyses of molecular data, plus detailed studies of plant morphology, and is represented in a Tree of Life. For those wishing to go deeper into this subject, see the work of Peter Stevens at the Missouri Botanical Garden: P. F. Stevens (2001 onwards), on his Angiosperm Phylogeny Website, www.mobot.org/MOBOT/research/APweb, accessed 31 August 2016.

14 The cucurbits, as they are known, are in the order Cucurbitales and share their phylogenetic grouping (the fabids) with another plant whose fruits (drupes) we also call berries – the fragrant bayberries (*Morella* or *Myrica* sp.), whose waxy coating was used in North America to make candles.

15 The citrus fruits are all members of the *Citrus* genus within the family Rutaceae, in the Sapindales order.

16 Attempts to eradicate the blackberry/bramble in areas of Australia, New Zealand and the United States, where it is listed as a noxious weed, are foiled by its deliciousness; it is widely cultivated, and continuing commercial imports make control difficult.

17 Anatoly Liberman, 'Monthly Etymology Gleanings for March 2015', OUPblog (1 April 2015), https://blog.oup.com; see also the entry in William Sayers, *Etymologies: Historical Notes on Culinary Terms* (Oxford, 2016).

18 See 'Rubus' in *The Plant List*, www.theplantlist.org, accessed 29 August 2016. The most common species of European blackberry is *Rubus fruticosus* or *plicatus*, while the raspberry is *Rubus idaeus*; the American species are *Rubus allegheniensis* and *Rubus idaeus* subspecies *strigosus*.

19 In Newfoundland, the berry is called 'bakeapple', a name that may derive from its taste, somewhat similar when ripe to a baked apple, or according to local lore, from the query by visiting French sailors who asked, 'What is this berry called?' or *La baie qu'appelle?*. In Quebec, the berry is known as *chicouté*.

20 Raspberries do, however, cross-pollinate, with the help of bees.

21 See 'Fragaria' in *The Plant List*, www.theplantlist.org, accessed 29 August 2016.

22 'Among others there is a very fine one with a sweetish taste, like that of the plantains (a fruits of the Indies) as white as snow, with leaves like those of the nettle, and it creeps up the trees and long the ground like ivy.' Samuel de Champlain, *The Works of Samuel de Champlain*, vol. II, ed. H. P. Biggar (Toronto, 1925), p. 177.

23 A spurious translation of the Ainu word but an effective advertising slogan; see http://haskap.ca/health-benefits, accessed 30 November 2016.

24 During the Bon Festival in Japan, seeds of *P. alkekengi* are sold as offerings to guide the souls of the deceased. They are toxic to mammals.

25 Such was its reputation that the Italian name *melanzane* was interpreted as *mala insana* – the 'mad apple' – though the eminent doctor Antonius Musa Brassavola, having enjoyed the plant stewed and fried by the ladies Isabella and Julia of Tarragon, disputed this. Nevertheless, Linnaeus dubbed the plant *Solanum insanum*; see Edward Lee Greene, *Landmarks of Botanical History*, Part II (Stanford, CA, 1983), pp. 688–9.

26 From 'Autumn Berries', *British Medical Journal*, II/1606 (1891), pp. 805–6.

27 George Arents Collection, The New York Public Library, 'Some Poisonous Berries', New York Public Library Digital Collections, https://digitalcollections.nypl.org, accessed 27 December 2018.

28 'Bryan on Scouting', *Scouting Magazine* blog, https://blog.scoutingmagazine.org, accessed 1 December 2018.

2 Berries in Mind

1 Ovid, *Metamorphoses*, ed. Frank Justus Miller and G. P. Goold, 3rd edn (Cambridge, MA, 1977), Book X, p. 71, www-loebclassics-com, accessed 1 July 2018.

2 Ibid., Book XLII, pp. 10–11.

3 The offering of a sweet fruit to stimulate desire appears to have a long history; see Lucretius Carus, Titus, et al., *De rerum natura* (Cambridge, MA, 1992), www-loebclassics-com, accessed 3 July 2018.

4 First published in 1934 and seemingly in print ever since, the image of the Strawberry fairy from *A Flower Fairy Alphabet* (London, 1934) has been reimagined into porcelain figurines, cross-stitch patterns, wooden puzzles and decoupage. The flower fairy in turn may be the model for the popular American rag doll Strawberry Shortcake, introduced into the crowded toyscape of the USA in 1979 by Kenner Products, and whose sweetness for children was enhanced by a special feature – the artificial aroma of strawberries.

5 M.S.S., 'A Hospital Blackberry Feast', from *The Prize for Girls and Boys* (London, 1880), p. 23.

6 In late autumn, blackberries do degenerate and become vulnerable to certain fungi, which are occasionally toxic.

7 Anonymous, *The Babes in the Wood: One of R. Caldecott's Picture Books* (London, 1880), available at www.gutenberg.org, accessed 24 June 2018.

8 John Swain also wrote a poem about bilberrying, somewhat less rollicking: 'But not for us would always smile the day; / For while we gather'd berries blue, the clouds / Would gather blackness, and toss out the storm! / And were we wretched then? I tell thee, friend, / There were not merrier children in the world!' John Swain, *The Tide of Even, and Other Poems* (London, 1877), pp. 204–5.

9 Henry David Thoreau, 'Huckleberries' [c. 1859], in *Wild Apples and Other Natural History Essays* (Athens, GA, 2002), p. 176.

10 Ibid., p. 187.

11 Ibid., pp. 192–3.

12 Ibid., p. 191.

13 Henry David Thoreau, *Wild Fruits: Thoreau's Rediscovered Last Manuscript*, ed. Bradley P. Dean (New York, 2000), p. 4.

14 Thoreau, 'Huckleberries', p. 194.

15 Ibid., p. 188.

16 'Their habitations are the groves, and the berries their diet.' The Latin text is *alimenta bacae*. Pliny the Elder, *The Natural History*, trans. John Bostock and H. T. Riley (London, 1855), www.perseus.tufts.edu, accessed 3 July 2018.

17 Thoreau, *Wild Fruits*, pp. 16–17.

18 Father Andrew White, a Jesuit missionary, describing Maryland in 1634 in *A Briefe Relation of the Voyage unto Maryland* (London, 1635), http://aomol.msa.maryland.gov, accessed 27 June 2018. In South America too,

particularly in Chile, fruit was so plentiful that, as Padre Alonso de Ovalle noted in 1641, 'one generally does not buy fruit, rather one is readily allowed to enter the orchards and eat all you wish', cited by Jim Stuart on his 'Eating Chilean' blog, www.eatingchile.blogspot.com, 14 November 2009.

19 Thoreau, *Wild Fruits*, p. 16.

20 William Bartram, *Travels Through North and South Carolina, Georgia, East and West Florida, the Cherokee Country . . . Together with Observations on the Manners of the Indians* (Philadelphia, PA, 1791), pp. 356–7.

21 Thoreau, *Wild Fruits*, p. 17. Thoreau's romantic rhapsody is somewhat spoiled by Charles Darwin's observation that in what were literally the ends of the earth, the 'vegetable diet of the Fuegians consisted chiefly of a fungus' and 'a few berries, chiefly of a dwarf arbutus' – not a paradisiacal diet. Robert FitzRoy, *Narrative of the Surveying Voyages of His Majesty's Ships Adventure and Beagle Between the Year 1826 and 1836*, vol. II (London, 1839), p. 185.

22 Ovid, *Metamorphoses*, Book VIII, pp. 452–3.

23 Thoreau, 'Huckleberries', pp. 190–91.

24 Robert Frost, 'Blueberries', in *North of Boston* (New York, 1915), pp. 56–63.

25 Ralph Waldo Emerson, 'Berrying', in *Poems* (Boston, MA, 1847), p. 64.

26 Edmund Spenser, Sonnet XLIII: 'Amoretti and Epithalamion' [1595], in *The Complete Works of Edmund Spenser*, ed. Alexander B. Grosart, vol. IV (London, 1882), p. 109.

27 James Orchard Halliwell, *The Nursery Rhymes of England* (London, 1886), no. 294.

28 The Chipewyan and the Iroquois also call the fruit 'heart-berry', only in partial acknowledgement of its shape. James Mooney, *Myths of the Cherokee* (Washington, DC, 1902), p. 260, available at www.gutenberg.org, accessed 30 June 2018.

29 Dr William Butler, quoted in Izaak Walton, *The Complete Angler, or the Contemplative Man's Recreation* (London, 1815), pp. 199–200.

30 It is the perfidious Iago who casts the doubt in Othello's mind:

Nay, but be wise: yet we see nothing done;
She may be honest yet. Tell me but this,
Have you not sometimes seen a handkerchief
Spotted with strawberries in your wife's hand?
(William Shakespeare, *Othello*, III/3).

31 Pedro Pineda, *A New Dictionary, Spanish and English and English and Spanish: Containing the Etimology, the Proper and Metaphorical Signification of Words, Terms of Arts and Sciences . . .* (London, 1741): 'Madróño, a sort of Fruit they have in Spain, like a Strawberry, eating whereof they say makes People drunk.'

32 Walter S. Gibson, 'The Strawberries of Hieronymus Bosch', *Cleveland Studies in the History of Art*, VIII (2003), p. 25. The *madroño* reportedly has an insipid taste, so that it gave a pleasure that was indeed fleeting.

33 Irish Traditional Music Archive, 'Ballad Sheet II Scrapbook, Part II', www.itma.ie, accessed 2 August 2018.

34 'Rose, stretching up / lifted her trembling arm / to pluck a mulberry from the branches / yet I did not see her pale arm' (author's translation). The poem was set to music by Frédéric d'Erlanger in 1895, and several verses were translated into English by Francis Charles Philips as 'Rose', but unfortunately not the verse quoted here. Victor Hugo, 'Vieille chanson du jeune temps', from *Les Contemplations* (Paris, 1856), available at www.poesie-francaise.fr, accessed 3 July 2018.

35 'Broadside Ballads', National Library of Scotland, https://digital.nls.uk, accessed 2 July 2018.

36 Alfred Perceval Graves, 'My Love's an Arbutus', in *Songs of Old Ireland* (1882), www.libraryireland.com, accessed 2 August 2018.

37 'She's the White Flower of the Blackberry', eighteenth-century Irish folksong, Kenneth Hurlstone Jackson, *A Celtic Miscellany: Translations from the Celtic Literatures* (London, 1951), no. 58.

38 Joyce Carol Thomas, 'Lubelle Berries', *The Black Scholar*, X/3–4: Black Literature (November/December 1978), p. 21.

3 Berries in the Hand

1 W. S. Coleman, *Our Woodlands, Heaths, and Hedges: A Popular Description of Trees, Shrubs, Wild Fruits, etc.: With Notices of Their Insect Inhabitants* (London, 1859), quoted in Henry David Thoreau, 'Huckleberries', in *Wild Apples and Other Natural History Essays* (Athens, GA, 2002), p. 43.

2 See Harriet V. Kuhnlein and Nancy J. Turner, 'Traditional Plant Foods of Canadian Indigenous Peoples: Nutrition, Botany and Use, Food and Nutrition', *History and Anthropology*, VIII (Amsterdam, 1991), p. 7.

3 'Dried berry cakes also were highly sought after by coastal First Nations and were one of the most important trade goods which the Gitksan and Wet'suwet'en transported over the Grease Trail to the coast to trade for eulachon grease and other products'. Scott Trusler and Leslie Main Johnson, '"Berry Patch" as a Kind of Place: The Ethnoecology of Black Huckleberry in Northwestern Canada', *Human Ecology*, XXXVI/4 (August 2008), pp. 553–68.

4 Mary Lockwood, 'Tundra Gathering', *Frontiers: A Journal of Women Studies*, XXIII/2: Indigenous Women (2002), pp. 33–5.

5 John Bennett and Susan Rowley, eds, 'Gathering', in *Uqalurait: An Oral History of Nunavut* (Montreal, 2004), p. 80.

6 Perhaps the Japanese fairy tale retold by Claudius Ferrand in 'Les Fraises de décembre' takes its inspiration from this practice. In the fable, the long-suffering Chrysanthemum is forced to search for strawberries in winter. Her search is in vain until her lament is heard by the goddess of winter, who magically reveals the red berries beneath the snow. Claudius Ferrand, *Fables et légendes du Japon* (Paris, 1903), pp. 99–107.

7 The bitter 'soapberries' of the West Coast (*Shepherdia canadensis*) are also transformed into a whipped confection, still served at family gatherings and more recently in upscale restaurants. See Kuhnlein and Turner, 'Traditional Plant Foods', p. 106.

8 Chantal Norrgard, 'From Berries to Orchards: Tracing the History of Berrying and Economic Transformation Among Lake Superior Ojibwe', *American Indian Quarterly*, XXXIII/1 (Winter 2009), pp. 33–61.

9 George W. Wood, 'The Wild Blueberry Industry – Past', *Small Fruits Review*, III/1–2 (2004), p. 12.

10 Trusler and Johnson, '"Berry Patch"', p. 556.

11 Norrgard, 'From Berries to Orchards', p. 49.

12 Rebecca T. Richards and Susan J. Alexander, *A Social History of Wild Huckleberry Harvesting in the Pacific Northwest*, USDA Forest Service, General Technical Report PNW-GTR-657 (Portland, OR, 2006), p. 9.

13 Lockwood, 'Tundra Gathering', p. 34.

14 In 1672 John Josselyn recorded that there were

> Bill-berries, two kinds, black and sky colored, which is more frequent . . . The Indians dry them in the sun and sell them to the English by the bushel, who make use of them instead of currence, putting of them into puddens, both boyled and baked, and into water gruel.
> Thoreau, 'Huckleberries', p. 182.

> Two hundred years later in 1883, the *North Wisconsin News* noted that the Ojibwe were supplying local townsfolk: 'A few blueberries have been brought into town this week, but was all purchased promptly by our citizens for home consumption, at a shilling a quart.' Trusler and Johnson, '"Berry Patch"', p. 40.

15 Richard Peters, quoted in Peter Hatch, 'Arcadian Dainties with a True Paradisiacal Flavor', *Twinleaf Journal Online* (1997), www.monticello.org, accessed 20 June 2018.

16 Thoreau, 'Huckleberries', pp. 190–93.

17 Wood, 'The Wild Blueberry Industry', p. 13.

18 National Park Service, *From Marsh to Farm: The Landscape Transformation of Coastal New Jersey*, www.nps.gov/parkhistory, accessed 3 July 2018.

19 S. W. Fletcher, *The Strawberry in North America: History, Origin, Botany, and Breeding* (New York, 1917), p. 59.

20 'La Fraise des quatre saisons', *L'Agriculture nouvelle* (17 May 1913), www.shw-woippy.net.

21 George M. Darrow, *The Strawberry: History, Breeding and Physiology* (New York, 1966), p. 17.

22 Henry Mayhew, *London Labour and the London Poor* (London, 1861), pp. 81, 85.

23 Daniel Lysons, *The Environs of London*, vol. II: *Part 2: County of Middlesex* (London, 1811), pp. 840–41.

24 David Harvey, 'Fruit Growing in Kent in the Nineteenth Century', *Archaeologia Cantiana*, LXXIX (1964), p. 104.

25 'Poudrette is neither more nor less than night-soil dried, and reduced to a powder. Poudrette, we understand, was first recommended by the celebrated Parmentier, about thirty years ago.' Patrick Neill, *Journal of a Horticultural Tour Through Some Parts of Flanders, Holland, and the North of France, in the Autumn of 1817* (Edinburgh, 1823), p. 367.

26 APUR (Atelier Paris d'urbanisme), *Évolution de la nature à Paris de 1730 à nos jours* (Note 122, February 2018), n.p., www.apur.org.

27 Neill, *Journal of a Horticultural Tour*, p. 436.

28 Lysons, *The Environs of London*, p. 444. The women who earned 3s. 6d. made about £12 in current British money (see Measuring Worth, www.measuringworth.com).

29 *The Saturday Magazine*, IV (January–June 1834), pp. 222–3, available at https://play.google.com/books, accessed 10 July 2018.

30 William Page, ed., *A History of the County of Hampshire*, vol. III (London, 1908), available at *British History Online*, www.british-history.ac.uk, accessed 1 March 2019.

31 Hampshire Archives, 'A Taste of Summer: Strawberry Growing in Hampshire' (3 May 2017), https://hampshirearchivesandlocalstudies. wordpress.com.

32 'Histoire de Woippy – La Fraise de Woippy' (Raconte-moi-Woippy)', www.shw-woippy.net, accessed 9 July 2018.

33 'The Strawberry Harvest', *Scientific American*, XIII/1 (1 July 1865), p. 2.

34 At a time when the average daily rate for women farm workers was about $1, this might be seen as good pay for a very hard day's work. Strawberries sold for $0.30 to $0.40 per quart. See United States Department of the Treasury, Bureau of Statistics, 'Special Report on Immigration: Accompanying Information for Immigrants . . . in the Year 1869–'70', Washington: G.P.O. (1871), https://catalog.hathitrust.org, accessed 9 July 2018.

35 Fletcher, *The Strawberry in North America*, p. 68.

36 National Park Service, *From Marsh to Farm*.

37 Captions to photographs by Lewis Hine, National Child Labor Committee Collection, Library of Congress, www.loc.gov, accessed 2 July 2018.

38 Linda Cullum, '"It was a woman's job, I 'spose, pickin' dirt outa berries": Negotiating Gender, Work, and Wages at Job Brothers, 1940–1950', *Newfoundland and Labrador Studies*, XXIII/2 (2008), p. 13.

39 'Strawberry Picker Checks of Sarcoxie, Missouri', *Nova Numismatics* (4 June 2011), www.novanumismatics.com.

40 Hampshire Archives, 'A Taste of Summer'.

41 SOPSE, 'Strawberry Train Exhibition, Westbury Manor Museum, Fareham', www.sopse.org.uk, accessed 2 July 2018.

42 Alison Campse, '100 Years of Berry Picking and Scottish Summers', *The Scotsman* (29 June 2016), www.scotsman.com.

43 Richard Moore-Colyer, 'Children's Labour in the Countryside during World War II: A Further Note', *Agricultural History Review*, XLIV/2 (2006), p. 332.

44 *Elles sont particulièrement demandées pour la récolte des fraises et des cerises. Ce sont des fruits fragiles qui nécessitent des mains habiles, délicates,* [They are particularly sought for strawberry and cherry picking. These fragile fruits demand skilled and delicate hands.] in Anne Le Nir, 'Les Italiennes, nouvelles esclaves des champs du sud de l'Italie', *RFI* (27 May 2015), www.rfi.fr.

45 In 2018 Spain recruited up to 16,000 female pickers. *Géopolis*, 'Récoltes des fraises: L'Espagne va recruter entre 13.000 et 16.000 Marocaines' (2 February 2018), http://geopolis.francetvinfo.fr; see also Salma Khouja, '"Dames de fraises, doigts de fée", l'enquête qui met en lumière le travail des saisonnières marocaines en Espagne', *HuffPost Maroc* (2 February 2018), www.huffpostmaghreb.com.

46 Juana Moreno Nieto, '"Faut-il des mains de femmes pour cueillir les fraises?" Dynamique de la gestion de la main-d'œuvre et du travail dans le secteur fraisier du périmètre irrigué du Loukkos (Maroc)', *Les Études et essais du Centre Jacques Berque*, XI (December 2012), available at www.researchgate.net, accessed 9 July 2018.

47 'Contextualizing Forced Labor in the Strawberry Industry', *Global Human Trafficking* (5 March 2018), https://u.osu.edu/osuhtblog.

48 P. M. Weston and M. L. Espir, 'Strawberry Pickers' Foot Drop', *British Medical Journal*, 11/6085 (1977), p. 520; S. Tanaka, 'Blueberry Rakers' Tendinitis', *New England Journal of Medicine*, CCCXXXI (25 August 1994), p. 552.

49 Helena Smith, 'Bangladeshi Fruit Pickers Shot at by Greek Farmers Win Human Rights Case', *The Guardian* (30 March 2017), available at www.theguardian.com.

50 'Everyman's right' is a literal translation of a Finnish-Swedish term (Finnish: *jokamiehen oikeus*; Swedish: *allemansrätt*).

51 See Swedish Environmental Protection Agency, 'Picking Flowers, Berries, Mushrooms, etc.', www.swedishepa.se, accessed 29 December 2018.

52 Finnish Forest Association, 'Participation in Forest-related Pursuits in Finland in 2010' (updated 2012), https://smy.fi/en, accessed 30 December 2018.

53 The Finnish berry picking industry is largely unregulated, and the Thai government restricted exit visas for berry pickers in 2017. See 'Thailand Cuts Number of Berry Pickers to Finland – After Last Year's Human Trafficking Scandal', *Uutiset* (27 May 2018), https://yle.fi/uutiset.

54 Lucy Hooker, 'The Strawberry-picking Robots Doing a Job Humans Won't', *BBC News* (25 May 2018), www.bbc.com/news.

55 The robots will, undoubtedly, be joined by the new 'U-Pick' armies who migrate once or twice a season to the country, not for economic reasons but to experience the pleasures of country life. In Wakayama, Japan, the Kishigawa Strawberry (Ichigo) train, decorated in red and white with strawberry cushions to take tourists to the greenhouses, has replaced the 'strawberry specials' that once rushed berries to market.

4 Garden Varieties

1 Olivier de Serre, *Le Théâtre d'agriculture et mesnage des champs* (Paris, 1605), pp. 576–7; Francis Bacon, 'Of Gardens', in *The Essayes or Counsels, Civill and Morall* (London, 1625), p. 276.

2 John Parkinson, *Paradisi in sole paradisus terrestris; or, A Garden of All Sorts of Pleasant Flowers Which our English Ayre Will Permitt to be Noursed . . .* (London, 1629), p. 526.

3 Thomas Hill, quoted in George M. Darrow, *The Strawberry: History, Breeding and Physiology* (New York, 1966), pp. 22–3.

4 Peter Hatch, 'Arcadian Dainties with a True Paradisiacal Flavor', *Twinleaf Journal Online* (1997), www.monticello.org, accessed 20 June 2018.

5 Parkinson, *Paradisi in sole*, p. 528.

6 Padre Alfonso de Ovalle, quoted in Darrow, *The Strawberry*, pp. 25–6.

7 Darrow, *The Strawberry*, p. 31.

8 The eighteenth-century pottle held about one litre or quart.

9 Amédée-François Frézier, quoted in Darrow, *The Strawberry*, pp. 31–4.

10 Philip Miller quoted ibid., p. 36.

11 S. W. Fletcher, *The Strawberry in North America: History, Origin, Botany, and Breeding* (New York, 1917), pp. 38–9.

12 Ibid., pp. 39–40.

13 Parkinson, *Paradisi in sole*, pp. 557–61, 571, 603.

14 Hence the name, *groseille à maquereau*, or mackerel currant.

15 Patrick Neill, *Journal of a Horticultural Tour Through Some Parts of Flanders, Holland, and the North of France, in the Autumn of 1817* (Edinburgh, 1823), pp. 466–7.

16 Books were available at the Falstaff Inn, care of Sir John Falstaff. It was, of course, his namesake who memorably opined in *Henry IV, Part 1*, Act II, Scene 4, 'If reasons were as plentiful as blackberries, I would give no man a reason upon compulsion, I.' *Gooseberry Growers' Register, or, An Account of the Different Gooseberry Shows Held in Lancashire, Cheshire, and Other Parts of the Kingdom, for the Year 1851 . . .* (Salford, 1851).

17 Charles Darwin, *The Variation of Animals and Plants under Domestication* (New York, 1894), vol. I, p. 378.

18 'Egton Bridge Gooseberry Show', www.egtongooseberryshow.org.uk, accessed 11 July 2018.

19 Catherine Parr Traill, *Studies of Plant Life in Canada: Wild Flowers, Flowering Shrubs, and Grasses* (Toronto, 1906), p. 161.

20 Hannah Glasse, *The Art of Cookery Made Plain and Easy Which Far Exceedeth Any Thing of the Kind Yet Published* (London, 1747), p. 118.

21 Henry David Thoreau, 'Huckleberries', in *Wild Apples and Other Natural History Essays* (Athens, GA, 2002), p. 43.

22 Robert S. Cox, *New England Pie: History Under a Crust* (Charleston, SC, 2015), p. 88.

23 Elizabeth White, quoted in National Parks Service, 'Whitesbog Village & Cranberry Bog', HALS (Historic American Landscape Survey) (Washington, DC, n.d.), p. 40.

24 Frederick Coville, *Experiments in Blueberry Culture*, USDA Bureau of Plant Industry, Bulletin 193 (Washington, DC, 1911), pp. 13–14.
25 J. Kim Kaplan, 'Blueberry Growing Comes to the National Agricultural Library', *Agricultural Research* (May–June 2011), pp. 13–15.
26 O. H. Barnhill, 'Growing the Blueberry, Queen of the Small Fruits', *San Francisco Examiner* (22 July 1923), cited in National Parks Service, 'Whitesbog Village and Cranberry Bog', p. 50.
27 Thoreau, 'Huckleberries', p. 188.
28 National Park Service, *From Marsh to Farm: The Landscape Transformation of Coastal New Jersey*, www.nps.gov, accessed 3 July 2018.
29 Cesar Rodriguez-Saona et al., 'Tracing the History of Plant Traits Under Domestication in Cranberries: Potential Consequences on Anti-herbivore Defences', *Journal of Experimental Botany*, LXII/8 (1 May 2011), pp. 2633–44.
30 Jonathan Roberts, *The Origins of Fruit and Vegetables* (New York, 2001), p. 17.
31 K. E. Hummer, Chad Finn and Michael Dossett, 'Luther Burbank's Best Berries', *Horticultural Science*, L/2 (February 2015), p. 207.
32 Luther Burbank, 'The Sunberry – A Production from the Wild; A New Food Plant From a Poisonous Family', in Luther Burbank et al., *Luther Burbank: His Methods and Discoveries and Their Practical Application* (New York, 1914).

5 Preserving the Harvest

1 Henry David Thoreau, 'Huckleberries', in *Wild Apples and Other Natural History Essays* (Athens, GA, 2002), p. 239.
2 From *De re coquinaria (On the Subject of Cooking): Apicius, Cooking and Dining in Imperial Rome*, trans. Joseph Dommers Vehling, available at www.gutenberg.org, accessed 22 July 2018.
3 'Black Huckleberry', USDA Plant Guide/Fact Sheet, https://plants.usda.gov, accessed 22 July 2018.
4 Gabriel Sagard and Roger Williams, quoted in Thoreau, 'Huckleberries', p. 181.
5 Terrence Scully, *The Viandier of Taillevent: An Edition of All Extant Manuscripts* (Ottawa, 1988), pp. 283, 296, 301.
6 Mulberries are not native to England but were introduced by the Romans.
7 John Gerard, *The Herball; or, Generall Historie of Plantes*, enlarged and amended by Thomas Johnson (London, 1636), p. 998.
8 Thomas Austin, ed., *Two Fifteenth-century Cookery-books* (London, 1888), p. 29.
9 Gerard, *The Herball*, p. 1,420.
10 Bartolomeo Scappi, *The Opera of Bartolomeo Scappi (1570): L'arte et prudenza d'un maestro cuoco*, trans. with commentary by Terence Scully (Toronto, 2008), pp. 247, 587.
11 François Massialot, *Nouvelle instruction pour les confitures, les liqueurs, et les fruits, avec la manière de bien ordonner un dessert . . .* [1692] (Paris, 1715). pp. 34–45, 147–79, 366–80, 450–55.
12 Gerard, *The Herball*, p. 1594.

13   Gervase Markham, *Countrey Contentments; or The English Huswife: Containing the Inward and Outward Vertues Which Ought to be in a Compleate Woman* (London, 1623), p. 110.

14   Hannah Glasse, *The Art of Cookery Made Plain and Easy Which Far Exceedeth Any Thing of the Kind Yet Published* (London 1747), pp. 231–2.

15   'I dare say, that every servant who can but read wilt be capable of making a tolerable good cook, and those who have the least notion of Cookery cannot miss of being very good ones.' Ibid., p. i. Glasse railed against those who were imposed on by a French 'booby', insisting they would do better with 'a good *English* cook'. Her preserves nevertheless echo those of Massialot.

16   And strangely, 'Elder-shoots in Imitation of Bamboo'; ibid., p. 207.

17   Ibid., p. 239.

18   Ibid., p. 222. Mayhew also describes the hot spiced elder wine sold by the glass in Covent Garden to working-class men and boys:

Along with each glass of hot elder wine is given a small piece of toasted bread. Some buyers steep this bread in the wine, and so imbibe the flavour. 'It ain't no good as I know on,' said an elder-wine seller, 'but it's the fashion, and so people must have it.' Henry Mayhew, *London Labour and the London Poor* (London, 1861), pp. 189–90.

19   Leo Tolstoy, *Anna Karenina* [1877], trans. Nathan Haskell Dole (New York, 1899), Part V, pp. 67–8.

20   E. F. Haskell, *The Housekeeper's Encyclopedia of Useful Information for the Housekeeper in All Branches of Cooking and Domestic Economy* (New York, 1864), p. 282. Haskell's book was translated into Japanese in 1876 as *Keizaishogaku Kaseiyoshi*. This influential book was taught in elementary schools and read by the public, contributing to the development of a Western notion of domestic economy in Meiji-era Japan.

21   Ibid., p. vi.

22   In his 1854 *A Shilling Cookery for the People*, Alexis Soyer, the redoubtable chef of the Reform Club in London, turned his attentions to the cuisine of the 'industrial class, the backbone of every free country'. As an envoy to Ireland in 1847, Soyer saw at first hand the effects of poverty and sought to 'cure a disease' through instruction in cookery. Fresh fruit – 'Almost all small farmers and cottagers have generally some kind of fruit to spare at the end of the season' – is recommended chiefly as an ingredient in preserves, and almost all recipes that call for fruit use jam. He does recommend a fresh strawberry salad, dressed with cinnamon, a bit of sugar, and tempered with a gill of brandy. Alexis Soyer, *A Shilling Cookery for the People* (London, 1854).

23   W. Hamish Fraser, *The Coming of the Mass Market* (London, 1981), p. 168.

24   Arthur Hill Hassall, *Food and its Adulterations; Comprising the Reports of the Analytical Sanitary Commission of 'The Lancet' for the Years 1851 to 1854 Inclusive* (London 1855), pp. 482–9.

25 'Royal Jam', *British Medical Journal*, 1/632 (8 February 1873), p. 151.

26 'National Fruit-supply', *British Medical Journal*, 1/1202 (12 January 1884), p. 75.

27 Frederick Keeble, 'Intensive Cultivation During the War', *Journal of the Royal Society of Arts*, LXVIII/3542 (8 October 1920), pp. 745–7.

28 'Jam and the WI During the Second World War', www.thewi.org.uk, accessed 25 July 2018.

29 'Le Coup jeune de Bonne Maman', *Capital* (9 October 2009), www.capital.fr.

30 Henry David Thoreau, *Wild Fruits: Thoreau's Rediscovered Last Manuscript*, ed. Bradley P. Dean (New York, 2000), p. 106.

31 Gerard, *The Herball*, p. 998.

32 Ibid., p. 175.

33 Ibid., p. 1274.

34 Maud Grieve, *A Modern Herbal* [1931] (New York, 1971), available at https://botanical.com, accessed 27 July 2018.

35 'Having been brought to the point of death by the gout, in the year 1750, but cured by eating wood-strawberries, he ate every season as much of this fruit as he could, and as his stomach would bear; by which means he not only escaped the gout entirely, but also from so doing derived more benefit than others from drinking mineral waters, and got rid of the scurvy which every year rendered him heavy.' Richard Pulteney, *A General View of the Writings of Linnaeus* (London, 1805), p. 563.

36 Grieve, 'Elder', *A Modern Herbal*, p. 269.

37 'Insanity from Strawberries', *The Washington Post* (8 June 1915), on the YesterYear Once More blog, https://yesteryearsnews.wordpress.com, accessed 28 July 2018

38 'The Baleful Strawberry', *The News* (11 June 1907), ibid.

39 Jacob Biggle, *The Biggle Berry Book* (Philadelphia, PA, 1911), p. 15.

40 Viburnic acid, from viburnum, was similar to valerianic or valeric acid, isolated from valerian, another long-used remedy, particularly for female troubles (it was preferred to alcohol and that other sheet-anchor of nineteenth-century medicine, opium). Theodore Shennan, 'Experimental Research into the Action of *Viburnum prunifolium* (Black haw)', *Edinburgh Medical Journal*, XLII (November 1896), pp. 404–17.

41 H. Nakaishi et al., 'Effects of Black Currant Anthocyanoside Intake on Dark Adaptation and VDT Work-induced Transient Refractive Alteration in Healthy Humans', *Alternate Medicine Review*, V/6 (2000), pp. 553–62.

42 E. Pappas and K. M. Schaich, 'Phytochemicals of Cranberries and Cranberry Products: Characterization, Potential Health Effects, and Processing Stability', *Critical Reviews in Food Science and Nutrition*, 49 (2009), pp. 741–81.

43 Bottom Line Inc., 'Berries Are Better than Drugs', https://bottomlineinc.com, accessed 1 August 2018.

44 Jacqueline B. Marcus, 'Vitamin and Mineral Basics: The ABCs of Healthy Foods and Beverages, Including Phytonutrients and Functional Foods', *Culinary Nutrition: The Science and Practice of Healthy Cooking* (2013).

6 The Global Berry

1 George M. Darrow, *The Strawberry: History, Breeding and Physiology* (New York, 1966), p. 162.

2 According to FAO statistics, world acreage in 2017 was 395,844 ha (978,152 ac); www.fao.org/faostat, accessed 2 January 2019.

3 The quantity of bananas grown in 2017 (113,918,763 tonnes) was over twelve times that of strawberries, and there are almost 100 times as many tonnes of apples: the FAO estimated 865,590,060 tonnes in 2017.

4 Faith Clark et al., 'Food Consumption of Urban Families in the United States with an Appraisal of Methods and Analysis', *Agriculture Information Bulletin*, No. 132 (October 1954), Home Economics Research Branch, Agricultural Research Service, United States Department of Agriculture.

5 Statista, 'Per Capita Consumption of Fresh Berries in the United States from 2000 to 2015 (In Pounds)', www.statista.com, accessed 2 August 2018.

6 U.S. Highbush Blueberry Council, 'Blueberry Consumption Set to Continue Climbing' (3 May 2017), www.blueberrycouncil.org.

7 Katie Morley, 'Berry Craze Sees Fruit Overtake Vegetables in Shoppers' Baskets', *The Telegraph*, 2 January 2019, www.telegraph.co.uk, accessed 10 June 2019.

8 Fresh Plaza, 'UK Farmers Expect Further Uplift of Berry Crops' (7 September 2018), www.freshplaza.com.

9 'Chinese Taste for Blueberries Creates Huge Market Demand', *China Daily* (20 April 2018), www.chinadaily.com.

10 'Strawberry Generation', *New York Times* (30 November 2008), https://schott.blogs.nytimes.com.

11 'Just How Green Are Polytunnels?', *The Independent* (15 June 2006), www.independent.co.uk.

12 Haygrove, a manufacturer of polytunnels of all descriptions, highlights its new farm in Yunnan, situated in the remote Xishuangbanna region, 'an area of almost undiscovered natural beauty which is more familiar to backpackers than berry-growers'; see www.haygrove.com/polytunnels. A recent televised Spanish crime drama, *Mar de plástico*, is set in a fictional community where the 'plastic sea' of greenhouses dominates the landscape.

13 In China, thin agricultural plastic 'usually gets shredded through tillage and thus contributes to the phenomenon known in China as the *baise wuran*, the "white pollution" that litters their landscape, endangers livestock, and pollutes rivers and lakes.' M. Ingman, M. V. Santelmann and B. Tilt, 'Agricultural Water Conservation in China: Plastic Mulch and Traditional Irrigation', *Ecosystem Health and Sustainability* (11 June 2015).

14 Stephen Vann, 'Gray Mold – A Silent Strawberry Nemesis', www.uaex.edu/publications, accessed 3 August 2018.

15 Environmental Working Group (EWG), 'Shoppers' Guide to Pesticides in Produce 2018', www.ewg.org/foodnews, accessed 4 August 2018.

16 'The share of organic produce in total produce purchases is varying strongly per country, from 2% in Australia and 5% in the Netherlands to 9% in the U.S. and 15% in Sweden', RaboResearch, 'World Fruit Map 2018: Global Trade Still Fruitful' (February 2018), https://research. rabobank.com/far/en/home/index.html.

17 Josh Freeman, 'Totally Impermeable Film – A New Plastic Mulch Option for 2016 Fumigation' (13 November 2015), http://nwdistrict.ifas.ufl.edu/ phag.

18 Francis Bacon, *Sylva Sylvarum; or, A Natural History, in Ten Centuries* (London, 1670), Century V, pp. 411, 91.

19 Tim Hornyak, 'Tomatoes, Melons, Cucumbers Grown on Thin Films', CNET (17 August 2011), www.cnet.com/news; see also 'New Technology Makes Agriculture Possible on Barren Land', *Tomodachi* (Autumn 2015), www.japan.go.jp.

20 Kiwi production was more than 4 million metric tonnes in 2016; Statista, 'Kiwi Production Worldwide from 2000 to 2016', www.statista.com, accessed 4 August 2018.

21 'Chinese Gooseberry Becomes Kiwifruit: 15 June 1959', *New Zealand History*, https://nzhistory.govt.nz, accessed 2 January 2019.

22 International Blueberry Organizaion (IBO), 'Irradiation for Peruvian Blueberries Part of Wider U.S. Market Access Talks, Says Industry Rep' (19 March 2018). www.internationalblueberry.org.

23 Mona Popa, 'Shelf-life Extension of Berries: Most Relevant Quality Parameters and New Techniques Used for Berries Processing', Bioatlas – 6th International Conference on Food and Tourism (26–7 May 2016), available at www.researchgate.net, accessed 4 August 2018.

24 Statistics available from PubMed, National Center for Biotechnology Information, U.S. National Library of Medicine, www.ncbi.nlm.nih.gov/ pubmed, accessed 2 August 2018.

25 'Superfood', *Oxford English Living Dictionary*, https://en.oxforddictionaries. com, accessed 5 August 2018.

26 Bill Gibb and Alli Kirker, 'Berry Sales in the UK are Being Boosted by Consumer Demand for Healthy Products', *Sunday Post* (17 June 2016), www.sundaypost.com. Demand continues to rise: in 2018 blueberry sales increased 14 per cent. See 'Berry Sales Boom in Year of Extremes for Fruit & Veg' (14 December 2018), www.thegrocer.co.uk.

27 Linus Pauling Institute, 'Flavonoids', https://lpi.oregonstate.edu/mic, accessed 5 August 2018.

28 The popularity of 'smoothies', a 'healthy' mix of fruits and liquids, has accounted for a rise in fresh and frozen fruit consumption since first being popularized in North America in the 1970s.

29 Prairie Berries, 'PurpleFuel Packed with Endless Potential',
    https://prairieberries.com, accessed 5 August 2018.
30 Ibid.
31 Global Healing Center, '12 Health Benefits of Acai Berries',
    www.globalhealingcenter.com, accessed 5 August 2018.
32 N. P. Seeram, M. Aviram and Y. Zhang, 'Comparison of Antioxidant
    Potency of Commonly Consumed Polyphenol-rich Beverages in the
    United States', *Journal Agricultural Food Chemistry*, LVI/4 (February 2008),
    pp. 1415–22.
33 Charles Bixler Heiser, *Of Plants and People* (Norman, OK, 1992), p. 106.
34 All fruits described in the archives of the Slow Food Foundation for
    Biodiversity, www.fondazioneslowfood.com, accessed 5 August 2018.
35 Valerie Shore, 'New Research Yields Berry Interesting Results',
    UVic News (1 March 2018), www.uvic.ca/news.
36 Roland Fumasi, senior fruit and vegetables analyst at Rabobank in
    Fresno, California, quoted by Eduardo Thomson in 'The World Wants
    Blueberries All the Time. Chile's Excited', *Bloomberg* (18 April 2018),
    www.bloomberg.com.
37 Henry David Thoreau, 'Huckleberries', in *Wild Apples and Other Natural
    History Essays* (Athens, GA, 2002), p. 5.

Select Bibliography

🌾

Anderson, Heather A., *Berries: A Global History* (London, 2018)

Biggle, Jacob, *The Biggle Berry Book* (Philadelphia, PA, 1911)

Blackburne-Maze, Peter, *Fruit: An Illustrated History* (London, 2002)

Burbank, Luther, *His Methods and Discoveries and Their Practical Application*, vol. VI (New York, 1914)

Coville, Frederick, *Experiments in Blueberry Culture*, USDA Bureau of Plant Industry, Bulletin 193 (Washington, DC, 1911)

Darrow, George M., *The Strawberry: History, Breeding and Physiology* (New York, 1966)

Darwin, Charles, *The Variation of Plants and Animals under Domestication*, vol. I (New York, 1894)

Fletcher, S. W., *The Strawberry in North America: History, Origin, Botany, and Breeding* (New York, 1917)

Forsell, Mary, *Berries: Cultivation, Decoration and Recipes* (New York, 1989)

Gerard, John, *The Herball, or, Generall Historie of Plantes* (London, 1636)

Glasse, Hannah, *The Art of Cookery Made Plain and Easy* . . . (London, 1747)

Gooseberry Growers' Register, or, An Account of the Different Gooseberry Shows Held in Lancashire, Cheshire, and Other Parts of the Kingdom, for the Year 1851 (Salford, 1851)

Grieve, Maud, *A Modern Herbal* [1931] (New York, 1971)

Grigson, Jane, *Jane Grigson's Fruit Book* (London, 1983)

Haskell, Mrs E. F., *The Housekeeper's Encyclopedia of Useful Information for the Housekeeper in All Branches of Cooking and Domestic Economy* . . . (New York, 1861)

Hassall, Arthur Hill, *Food and its Adulterations; Comprising the Reports of the Analytical Sanitary Commission of 'The Lancet' for the Years 1851 to 1854 Inclusive* (London, 1855)

Kuhnlein, Harriet V., and Nancy J. Turner, 'Traditional Plant Foods of Canadian Indigenous Peoples: Nutrition, Botany and Use, Food and Nutrition', *History and Anthropology*, VIII (Amsterdam, 1991)

Maril, Lee, *Savor and Flavor: Berries in Fact and Fancy* (New York, 1944)

Massialot, François, *Nouvelle instruction pour les confitures, les liqueurs, et les fruits, avec la manière de bien ordonner un dessert* . . . (Paris, 1715)

Mayhew, Henry, *London Labour and the London Poor* (London, 1861)

National Park Service, *From Marsh to Farm: The Landscape Transformation of Coastal New Jersey*, www.nps.gov/parkhistory

—, 'Whitesbog Village and Cranberry Bog', Historic American Landscape Survey (HALS) (Washington, DC, n.d.)

National Research Council (U.S.) Advisory Committee on Technology Innovation, *Lost Crops of the Incas: Little-known Plants of the Andes with Promise for Worldwide Cultivation* (Washington, DC, 1989)

Parkinson, John, *Paradisi in sole paradisus terrestris; or, A Garden of All Sorts of Pleasant Flowers Which our English Ayre Will Permitt to be Noursed . . .* (London, 1629)

Root, Waverley, *Food* (New York, 1986)

Serres, Olivier de, *Le Théâtre d'agriculture et mesnage des champs* (Paris, 1605)

Seymour, Tom, *Nuts and Berries of New England: Tips and Recipes for Gatherers from Maine to the Adirondacks to Long Island Sound*, Falcon Guides (Guildford, CT, 2013)

Snow, Barbara, and David Snow, *Birds and Berries: A Study of an Ecological Interaction* (London, 1988)

Summers, Julie, *Jambusters: The Story of the Women's Institute in the Second World War* (London, 2013)

Thoreau, Henry David, *Wild Apples and Other Natural History Essays* (Athens, GA, 2002)

—, *Wild Fruits: Thoreau's Rediscovered Last Manuscript*, ed. Bradley P. Dean (New York, 2000)

Traill, Catherine Parr, *Studies of Plant Life in Canada: Wild Flowers, Flowering Shrubs, and Grasses* (Toronto, 1906)

Wallace, Alfred Russel, 'The Colours of Plants and the Origin of the Colour-sense', in *Tropical Nature and Other Essays* (London, 1878)

Wilson, C. Anne, *The Book of Marmalade: Its Antecedents, Its History and Its Role in the World Today* (Philadelphia, PA, 1999)

Associations and Websites

AGRICULTURAL MARKETING RESOURCE CENTER
www.agmrc.org

ANGIOSPERM PHYLOGENY WEBSITE
www.mobot.org/MOBOT/research/APweb

BIODIVERSITY HERITAGE LIBRARY
www.biodiversitylibrary.org

EGTON BRIDGE GOOSEBERRY SHOW
www.egtongooseberryshow.org.uk

FRESH FRUIT PORTAL
www.freshfruitportal.com

THE GROCER
www.thegrocer.co.uk

'HISTOIRE DE WOIPPY – LA FRAISE DE WOIPPY' (RACONTE-MOI-WOIPPY)
www.shw-woippy.net

INTEGRATED TAXONOMIC INFORMATION SYSTEM (ITIS)
www.itis.gov

IOS PRESS, *Journal of Berry Research*
www.iospress.nl/journal/journal-of-berry-research

NEW ZEALAND KIWIFRUIT GROWERS (NZKGI)
www.nzkgi.org.nz

THE PACKER
www.thepacker.com

THE PLANT LIST
www.theplantlist.org

RABOBANK, 'RABORESEARCH'
https://research.rabobank.com

SWEDISH ENVIRONMENT PROTECTION AGENCY
www.swedishepa.se

UNITED NATIONS, FOOD AND AGRICULTURE ORGANIZATION, FAOSTAT
www.fao.org/faostat

UNITED STATES DEPARTMENT OF AGRICULTURE, NATURAL RESOURCES
CONSERVATION SERVICE: PLANTS DATABASE
https://plants.sc.egov.usda.gov

U.S. CRANBERRIES
www.uscranberries.com

U.S. HIGHBUSH BLUEBERRY COUNCIL
www.blueberrycouncil.org

WIKIPEDIA: BERRY
https://en.wikipedia.org/wiki/Berry

WIKIPEDIA: LIST OF CULINARY FRUITS
https://en.wikipedia.org/wiki/List_of_culinary_fruits

Acknowledgements

My thanks to all those who have made their images available online to be enjoyed and re-used, particularly the museums and archives. In writing about cultural history, it is often images that provide the direction for research. My thanks as well to the great libraries of the world who have made so many books freely accessible to readers. The contributors to the global digital library – the Internet Archive, the Biodiversity Heritage Library, the Hathi Trust, Gallica and the many university libraries – have inaugurated a new world of digital scholarship unimagined even a decade ago. The oversight of colleagues is equally essential, and my gratitude to those who helped me navigate the perplexing world of berries. My particular thanks to David Wees, Associate Director of the Farm Management and Technology programme at Macdonald Campus, McGill University, who reviewed the botany of berries (though any mistakes are my own); to Deborah Buszard, Deputy Vice-Chancellor and Principal of the University of British Columbia's Okanagan campus, and a strawberry breeder, who warned me that berries are a complicated subject; and to Nancy Turner and Fiona Hamersley Chambers, at the School of Environmental Studies at the University of Victoria, who shared their enthusiasm for wild fruits and Indigenous knowledge. Finally, my thanks to Henry David Thoreau, whose delight in the humble fruits of field and forest lives on in his joyous prose.

Photo Acknowledgements

The author and publishers wish to express their thanks to the below sources of illustrative material and/or permission to reproduce it. Some locations of artworks are also given below, in the interests of brevity:

From Aesop and V. S. Vernon Jones, trans., *Aesop's Fables* (London and New York, 1912), courtesy The New York Public Library: p. 68; The Agricultural Research Service, USDA: pp. 93 (photo Keith Weller), 164 (photo Ken Hammond); The Art Institute of Chicago: p. 74; Boston Public Library: pp. 49, 79, 142; photo Jannis Brandt/Unsplash: p. 157; The British Library of Political and Economic Science, LSE: p. 81; The British Museum, London: pp. 16, 34, 60, 61, 65, 75, 80, 86, 98, 133, 134, 144; The Cleveland Museum of Art, OH: p. 26; Cornell University Library, Ithaca, NY: p. 122; from Denis Diderot and Jean Le Rond d'Alembert, eds, *Recueil de planches, sur les sciences, les arts libéraux, et les arts méchaniques*, vol. III (Paris, 1763), courtesy Smithsonian Libraries, Washington, DC: p. 131; from Amédée-François Frézier, *A Voyage to the South-sea, and along the Coasts of Chili and Peru, in the Years 1712, 1713, and 1714* (London, 1735), courtesy Getty Research Institute, Los Angeles, CA: p. 101; from Joseph Gaertner, *De Fructibus Et Seminibus Plantarum* (Stuttgart, 1788), courtesy Peter H. Raven Library, Missouri Botanical Garden, St. Louis, MO: p. 12; photo Wouter Hagens: p. 57; Imperial War Museum, London: p. 92; Library of Congress, Prints and Photographs Division, Washington, DC: pp. 9, 18, 88, 89, 90, 103, 117, 121, 138, 140, 141, 143, 147; from John Lindley, ed., *Pomological Magazine* (London, 1828–30), courtesy UMass Amherst Libraries: pp. 104 (vol. II), 110 (vol. I); Jane Wells Webb Loudon, *British Wild Flowers* (London, 1846), courtesy Smithsonian Libraries, Washington, DC: p. 27; from *Luther Burbank's Bounties from Nature to Man* (Chicago, IL, 1911), courtesy Sloan Foundation, Library of Congress, Washington, DC: p. 124; Museo Archeologico Nazionale di Napoli: p. 129; Museo Nacional del Prado, Madrid: pp. 63, 64; photo NASA Earth Observatory: p. 161; Nasjonalmuseet, Oslo: p. 46; The National Agricultural Library, USDA, Beltsville, MD: pp. 106, 163; The National Archives at College Park, MD: pp. 95, 145; National Galleries Scotland, Edinburgh: p. 48; National Gallery of Art, Washington, DC: pp. 73, 83; The New York Public Library: pp. 41, 45; photo courtesy Orange County Archives, Santa Ana, CA: p. 126; Claude Paradin, *Devises Heroïques* (Lyon,

Index

Abenaki 72
Aboriginal 38, 174
açai berries 10, 23, 173
Ainu 36, 171
akutaq ('Eskimo ice cream') 75, 77
Algonquin 72
apomixis 26
Appert, Nicolas, French *confiseur* 140, 180
anthocyanin *see* phytochemicals
antioxidant *see* phytochemicals
Arbutus unedo see strawberry tree
Arcadia 44–6, 55–6, 62–3
asterids 32–6
aubergines 38, 124
Australia 38, 128, 167, 174

'Babes in the Woods' 50
Bacon, Francis 97–8, 165–6
Ball, Kathryn, *Viscum album* 19
barberries *see* berberries
Barker, Cicely Mary, British artist 48
Bartram, William 55–6
Baucis and Philemon 56
bearberries 35, 73
Beecher, Henry Ward, American preacher and food critic 104–5
belladonna 38, *40*, 41, 123
berberries 23, 97, 105, 128, 132, 136
Bergman, Ingmar 66
Biggle, Jacob, American berry grower 151–2, 163

bilberries 8, 22, 32, *34*, 50, 66, 71–2, 94
Bilberry Sunday (Lughnasa) 66
birds 14–18, *16*, 20–21, 36, 41, 58, 62, 72, 125
blackberries 8, 13–14, 17, *18*, 21, 24–5, 27, 29, 58–60, 62, 67, 148, 162, 167–9, 171
    Colombian giant (*zarzamora*) 99, 173
    illnesses associated with 150–51
    Lubelle, tale of 69
    picking *8*, 48–50, *49*, 69, 72, 78, 90, 92
    preserving 137, 139
    varieties *106*, 120–21, 124–5, *122*, *124*
Blaigowrie (Scotland) 91, *92*
blueberries 7, 32, 35, 51, *52–3*, 58, 66, 72, 76, 78–9, 175
    Andean (*mortiño*) 128, 173–4
    blueberry culture 113–16, *114*
Bosch, Hieronymus, *The Garden of Earthly Delights* 62–4, *63*, *64*
Boy Scouts 40–41, *41*
boysenberry 125–6
Bradbury, Ray 8
brambles 24–7, *27*, 29, 45, 58, 99, 120
    parable 67–9, *68*
    remedies 149–50
Burbank, Luther, American plant breeder 120–25, *121*
Butler, William, English physician 61

Index

Caldecott, Randolph 50
Champlain, Samuel de 32, 179
Chelsea Physic Garden 29
Cherokee 55, 59
children 13, 40, 59, 112, 124, 133
    association with berries 46–54,
    48
    labour 85–93, 85, 88, 89, 90
    National Child Labor Committee
    87
    picking 49, 51, 54, 71–3, 73, 77–8,
    94, 118–19, 119
China 35, 38, 156, 160, 162, 167–8, 171
Chinese gooseberries see kiwifruit
cloudberries 9, 25, 27, 72–3, 94–5,
    128, 148
Cobbett, William 82
colour in berries 15–18
confiseur 130–32, 131, 134, 140
cornel-cherries 45, 56, 57, 105
costermongers 80–82, 81, 142
Coville, Frederick Vernon, botanist
    113, 113–16, 125, 181
Cranach, Lucas the Elder, The Golden
    Age 46
cranberries 10, 32, 35, 72–3, 78–9,
    148, 156, 158, 166, 168
    cranberry culture 114–20, 117,
    118–19
    health benefits 148, 155, 171
    picking 87–9, 89, 92, 93, 94
    preserving 75, 120, 128, 140, 169
'Cries of London' 80–81, 83
crowberries 9, 20, 32, 72
Cruikshank, Isaac, 'Folkstone
    Strawberries . . .' 86
currants 35, 37, 72, 82, 105, 106, 107,
    128, 137, 139–40, 156
    black 9, 35, 62, 12, 134, 148, 152
    red 9, 35, 62, 98, 106, 136–7, 143,
    150
    remedies 105, 130, 150, 152, 152,
    155, 171

Darrow, George, American
    horticulturist 125, 156

Darwin, Charles 14, 109–11
Delany, Mary 'Black Whortle or
    Bilberries' 34
Devil, the 38, 47, 47, 49, 67, 69–70,
    93
dewberries 25
Driscoll's, American berry growers
    167, 169, 181–2
Duchesne, Antoine Nicolas,
    Histoire naturelle des fraisiers 102,
    105, 180

elderberries 10, 15, 36, 41, 70, 128,
    137, 150, 153, 154
Emerson, Ralph Waldo, 'Berrying'
    58–9
ethanol 21
Evelyn, John 150
'Everyman's Right' 94–5

'fen berry' (small cranberry) 130
Fisher, Ellen Thayer, Blackberries
    18
Forbes, Elizabeth Adela, Blackberry
    Gathering 8
Frézier, Amédée-François, French
    gardener 100–102, 180
Frost, Robert, 'Blueberries' 58
'fruiticeutical' 36
'functional foods' 170–71

Gaertner, Joseph, De fructibus et
    seminibus plantarum 12
Gerard, John, Herball 129, 134, 142,
    148–50
Gitksan 72
Glasse, Hannah 112, 135–6, 138,
    180
goji berry 10, 171, 172, 182
Golden Age see Arcadia
goldenberry 38
gooseberries 9, 17, 35–6, 62, 70, 72,
    82, 91, 98, 105, 106, 110, 111–12,
    128, 130, 142, 156
    Clubs 108–10, 180
    Fool 105, 112

'Old Gooseberry' (the Devil)
69
preserving 111, 132–4, 136, 138,
140, 143
grapes 8, 11, 17, 23–4, 44, 56, 62, 67,
77, 127–30, *129*, 132, 157
Grieve, Maud, *A Modern Herbal*
150–3, 181

Haida 32, 72
Hall, Henry, American cranberry
grower 116, 180
haskap berries 9, 36, 171–2
Haskell, Mrs, *The Housekeeper's
Encyclopedia* 139–40
Hassall, Dr Arthur Hill 142–4
Heaney, Seamus, 'Blackberry-
picking' 69
Hesiod 44
hesperidium 12, 23
Hill, Thomas, *The Gardener's Labyrinth*
99
Hine, Lewis, American photographer
87–9, *88*, *89*
Hokusai, Katsushika, *Mozu ruri
yuki-no-shita hebi-ichigo 16*
holly 41, 67
Homer, Winslow
Gathering Wild Blackberries 49
Berry Pickers 73
huckleberries 8, 32, 43, 50–51, 60,
72, 76, 78, 112, 115, 175
Huckleberry Finn 51
'huckleberry people' 56, 58
Hugo, Victor, 'Vieille chanson
du jeune temps' 65–6
Humphreys, Henry Noel,
'Dewberry, Common Bramble
or Blackberry, Arctic of Dwarf
Crimson Bramble, Cloudberry'
27
Hurons 128

Inuit 35, 72, 74–5, 128
Iroquois 72, *75*
ivy 41, 44

jam-making
domestic *135*, 136, *137*, *138*, 138–9,
139, *140*, *144*, *145*, *146*, 173
industrial 141–8, *142*, *147*
Japan 28, 36, 94, 156, *165*, 166, 171
Jefferson, Thomas 100
John Moir & Son 142, *142*
Johnson, Eastman, *The Cranberry
Harvest, Island of Nantucket*
118–19
Jussieu, Antoine de 100, 180
Jussieu, Bernard de 102

Keens, Michael, British strawberry
grower 102–3, 180
kiwifruits (kiwis) 10, 35, 156, 167–8,
168, 182
Knott, Walter, American berry
grower 125–6, 181
Knott's Berry Farm 126, *126*
kutjera (bush tomato) 38, 128, 174,
174

Le Moyne de Morgues, Jacques
'Strawberry' *98*
lingonberries 32, 94
Linnaeus, Carolus 11, 14, 150–51,
155, 180
loganberry 125, 181
'love in a cage' (Chinese lantern
plant) 38, *39*
Lucretius 45
lulo (little orange) 174

madroño see strawberry tree
Markham, Gervase, *Countrey
Contentments, or The English Huswife*
134–5
Mason jar 141, 180
Massialot, François, *Nouvelle instruction
pour les confitures* 130–35, 179
Miller, Philip 29, 100
mistletoe 15, *19*, 20, 41
mulberries 9, 14, 29, *33*, 41, 55,
62, 64–5, *65*, 105, 107, 127,
129–30, 132

picking 65, *82*
preserving 127, 133
mycorrhizal fungi 32

Natchez 72
New Zealand 35, 38, 167–8, *168*, 170
Newfoundland 7, 25, 32, 90, 116
nightshade berries 38, 121, 123–4, 171
Northwest Coast (North America)
    25, 32, 72–3, 116, 125, 174

Ojibwe 76
organic berries 165, 169, 175
Orpheus 44
Othello and Desdemona 62
Ovid (Publius Ovidius Naso) 44–5

Paris 80, 82–6, 101–2, 108, 133, 147
Paris green *see* pesticides
Parkinson, John, *Paradisi in sole . . . 96*,
    98–9, 105
Peale, Sarah Miriam, *Basket of Berries*
    153
pemmican 74, *76*, 128, 172
pepo 11–12, 23
pesticides *162*, 162–5, *163*, 169, 175
phytochemicals
    anthocyanin 17–18, 155, 170,
        173
    antioxidant 154–5, 170–71,
        173
    carotenoids 17
    polyphenols (phenolic acids)153,
        170–71
plastic
    clamshell 169, 175
    plasticulture 93, 156, *161*, 165, 167,
        175, 182
    polytunnel 161–2
Pliny the Elder 54, 149
poisonous berries 38–42
polyploidy 28
polyphenols *see* phytochemicals
polytunnel *see* plastic
Potin, Félix, French grocer 147, 181
pottles *80*, 81, 84, 100, 105, 142, 151

Prokudin-Gorskii, Sergei
    Mikhailovich, *Peasant Girls 138*
Pyramus and Thisbe 64
Rackham, Arthur, *The Fir-tree and the
    Bramble 68*
raspberries 8, *9*, 20, 24–6, 29, 67,
    72, *77*, 81–2, 105, *106*, 107, 120–21,
    122, 132, *153*, 156–7, 159, 167–9, 171
    picking 84, 92, 94
    preserving 133–4, 137, 139–40,
        143, 145–6
ratafia *133*, 134
robot pickers 95
rosids 23–9
Russia 28, 49, 138–9, 171

Sagard, Gabriel, French missionary
    128
salal berries 32, 72, 174
salmonberries 9, 25, 78
Sami 35
saskatoon berries *see* serviceberries
Scappi, Bartolomeo, *Opera dell'arte
    del cucinare* 130, 179
sea buckthorn 15, 171
Serres, Olivier de, *Le Théâtre
    d'agriculture et mesnage des champs* 97
serviceberries 29, 60, 72, 172–3
Shakespeare, William 62
shipping 25, 79, 103, 141, 156, 166–7,
    169
    air 169
    rail 79–80, 84–6, 91, 166, *167*
    sea 79, 166, 169
slave labour 87, 95
snake 47, *47*, 62, 69
snowberry 14, 32
soilless cultivation *165*, 165–6,
    182
Solanum centrale see kutjera
Spenser, Edmund 59
strawberries 8, 10, 13, *13*, *16*, 17,
    20–21, 24–5, 28–9, *30–31*, *33*,
    47, 50–51, 55–6, 59–62, *60*, *61*,
    61–5, 72, 80–81, *83*, 107
    'blood' strawberries 93

Chilean strawberry 99–102, *101*
consumption 129–30, 132, 142,
    151–2, 156–60, *159*
cultivation 97–105, *104*, *106*, 122,
    146, 161, *164*, 165–6, *165*, 168
picking 44, 46–7, 85, *85*, 87–8,
    90–4, *95*, 96, 166
preserving 133–5, *137*, 139–40,
    143, 147
illness associated with 151–2
remedies 98, 149–52, 155, 171
'Strawberry Generation' (China)
    160
'Strawberry Specials' (railcars)
    85, 166
tokens 91
Virginia strawberry 29, 99, 102–3
strawberry tree (*madroño*) 10, 35, *36*,
    44, 46, 62–3, *64*, 66–7, 105
sunberry *see* wonderberry
'superfruit' 170–72, 174, 182

thimbleberries 25, 58
Thoreau, Henry David 7, 9, 22, 43–4,
    50–58, 72, 78–9, 112, 116, 127,
    148, 155, 175–6
Tolstoy, Leo 138
tomatoes 11, 17, 38, 123, 171, 174
Traill, Catherine Parr, Canadian
    author and gardener 111, *111*

varenye (Russian preserves) *137*,
    137–9, *138*, *139*
Vasnetsov, Apollinary, *Making Jam*
    139
Venus 46, 59
Virgil, Roman poet 47
Virgin Mary 47, 59, *60*
vitamins 154

Wallace, Alfred Russel 14–15
Watson, Thomas, after Sir Joshua
    Reynolds, *The Strawberry Girl* 48
Wet'suwet'en 72
whortleberries 15, *34*, 128, 130, 139
White, Elizabeth 114–16, 181

White, Joseph, *Cranberry Culture* 117
Whitesbog, New Jersey *114*, 115–17
Williams, Roger 128, 179
Wilson, James, American strawberry
    grower 103–5, 180
'Winter Supplies, The', *Woman's World*
    141
wolfberry *see* goji berry
women
    marketing *83*, 84, *86*
    picking 71–3, 78, 86–94, *92*, 119
    preserving 136, 138–9, *141*, *143*,
        146, 148
    Women's Institute, Britain 146
    Women's Land Army 146
wonderberry 121, 123, *123*, 181

Yakima 72
Youngberry 125, 181